THE
SEAFISH
COOKBOOK

THE
SEAFISH
COOKBOOK

SUSAN HICKS

HAMLYN

Photography by David Burch
Decorative illustrations by Gay John Galsworthy
Diagrams by Roberta Colegate-Stone

The publishers would like to thank the following for lending
the crockery shown in the photographs: Covent Garden
Kitchen Supplies, David Mellor, Reject China Shops,
Strangeways. Thanks are also due to J. Sainsbury plc for
providing the transparency used on page 39 and to Chalmers &
Gray Fishmongers of London for allowing us to photograph
their premises, as shown on page 34.

The author would like to thank the Sea Fish Industry
Authority for their co-operation and help in making this book
possible. In particular, I would like to acknowledge the
enthusiasm and help of Carolyn Cavele of their London office.
I should also like to thank Stephanie Hallin of Hamlyn
Publishing for her expertise in editing this book.

Published 1986 by Hamlyn Publishing
Bridge House, London Road, Twickenham, Middlesex

ISBN 0 600 32604 7

Set in Monophoto Goudy Old-Style by
Tameside Filmsetting Ltd
Printed in Spain by Cayfosa. Barcelona
Dep. Leg. B-3803 - 1986

Contents

Introduction

Fish, fabulous fish! Fish is endlessly fascinating for the imaginative cook, the fastest of fast foods, and the most nutritious for those with little time for culinary adventures.

For as long as I can remember, I have loved the sea. I started life in Grimsby and as a very small child on my first outing to the fish market the wonderful sea-fresh aroma of fish, and the clatter and bustle of the fishermen sorting out their catch, made a strong and lasting impression. A little later, I can remember my father buying two stones of mussels. The bottom fell out of the cardboard box in the middle of a busy cobbled street, producing a major traffic jam while my father and I scrambled to pick up all the mussels. We walked on nonchalantly by the hooting lorry drivers absolutely weighed down by bulging pockets full of mussels! My mother used to wait in fear and trepidation for my father's return from these expeditions.

Now I live on a beautiful island in the Scillies where my love and passion for seafood has continued. I have so many memories of wonderful fish suppers. The gleaming mackerel that seemed to jump from the sea into my pan; grey mullet barbecued on the beach; huge pots of fish soup to warm the late autumn evenings; and freshly cooked warm lobster consumed with delicious, tiny new potatoes just dug out of the ground. Wonderful memories, and recipes which I would like to share with you.

We have a fishing industry and marketing system geared towards bringing us a wealth of the freshest possible fish, yet compared to many countries we eat precious little of this natural and delicious food. Why is this?

Fortunately, however, a new wave of fish enthusiasm is at last sweeping the country as we become more discerning and healthy in our attitudes to food and lifestyle. For many people there is still an air of mystery about fish, and there seems to be a 'fear of fish'. Perhaps we have become distanced and numbed from real food and, at the same time, lulled into an acceptance of scrubbed and graded food sold to us in uniform packages and totally devoid of its original character and taste.

Yet, in the time I have been presenting fish cookery on television and writing this book, I have been thoroughly cheered by the fantastic response and interest from people ranging from absolute beginners, fish fans who want to know more about preparation and cooking methods, to real fish experts.

I do hope that this book, with its practical and comprehensive guide to all aspects of buying and preparing seafood, and recipes ranging from simple and new ideas to the favourite classics, will appeal to and inspire all lovers, or potential lovers, of fish. Above all, enjoy your fish!

Smoked Fish Mousse (page 69) and Grilled Fish with Pesto (page 121)

Useful Facts and Figures

Notes on metrication

In this book quantities are given in metric and Imperial measures. Exact conversion from Imperial to metric measures does not usually give very convenient working quantities and so the metric measures have been rounded off into units of 25 grams. The table below shows the recommended equivalents.

Ounces	Approx g to nearest whole figure	Recommended conversion to nearest unit of 25
1	28	25
2	57	50
3	85	75
4	113	100
5	142	150
6	170	175
7	198	200
8	227	225
9	255	250
10	283	275
11	312	300
12	340	350
13	368	375
14	396	400
15	425	425
16 (1 lb)	454	450
17	482	475
18	510	500
19	539	550
20 ($1\frac{1}{4}$ lb)	567	575

Note: When converting quantities over 20 oz first add the appropriate figures in the centre column, then adjust to the nearest unit of 25. As a general guide, 1 kg (1000 g) equals 2.2 lb or about 2 lb 3 oz. This method of conversion gives good results in nearly all cases, although in certain pastry and cake recipes a more accurate conversion is necessary to produce a balanced recipe.

Liquid measures The millilitre has been used in this book and the following table gives a few examples.

Imperial	Approx ml to nearest whole figure	Recommended ml
$\frac{1}{4}$ pint	142	150 ml
$\frac{1}{2}$ pint	283	300 ml
$\frac{3}{4}$ pint	425	450 ml
1 pint	567	600 ml
$1\frac{1}{2}$ pints	851	900 ml
$1\frac{3}{4}$ pints	992	1000 ml (1 litre)

Spoon measures All spoon measures given in this book are level unless otherwise stated.

Can sizes At present, cans are marked with the exact (usually to the nearest whole number) metric equivalent of the Imperial weight of the contents, so we have followed this practice when giving can sizes.

Oven temperatures

The table below gives recommended equivalents.

	C	F	Gas
Very cool	110	225	$\frac{1}{4}$
	120	250	$\frac{1}{2}$
Cool	140	275	1
	150	300	2
Moderate	160	325	3
	180	350	4
Moderately hot	190	375	5
	200	400	6
Hot	220	425	7
	230	450	8
Very hot	240	475	9

Note: When making any of the recipes in this book, follow only one set of measures as they are not interchangeable.

Accent on Health

How marvellous that such a delicious and fresh source of food as fish is also very good for you! You can enjoy as much fish as you like with the benefit of knowing that fish is nutritionally as near a perfect food as you are likely to find. Research suggests that eating fish a couple of times a week may actually lower cholesterol in the blood, and that may help to prevent heart disease.

Fish is a rich source of protein, vitamins and minerals. It contains very little carbohydrate, and what little fat there is in fish is unsaturated. Oily varieties, such as herring and mackerel, provide an excellent source of vitamins A and D, which are so essential for good health.

The flesh of white fish particularly is easily digested and, provided it is not cooked with floury sauces, or fried in batter, is ideal for those on gluten-free or diabetic diets.

There simply could not be a better food than fish for children. There are some inviting recipes in this book designed to appeal to youngsters – give them fish and they will be getting the essential raw materials for building flesh and muscle during their growing years.

For the adult, too, this superb nutritional package will feed, maintain and repair the body through to old age – without all those extra calories contained in other foods.

The chart on page 11 spells out the facts and figures.

And, in general terms, fish are made up of:

Moisture	65–85 per cent
Protein	15–25 per cent
Fats	0.1–22 per cent
Minerals	0.8–2 per cent

For all those concerned with healthy living and eating, fish offers yet further advantages. We can all enjoy seafood in the safe knowledge that it has not yet succumbed to the interference of intensive farming methods: no hormone growth producers, antibiotics, herbicides, pesticides, and so on should be present in seafood. From every point of view fish should take pride of place in our diets as a truly superior food.

THE NUTRITIONAL VALUE OF FISH

*Analysis per ounce based on raw edible portions of flesh.						
	Cod or Haddock	Herring	Beef	Lamb	Pork	Chicken
Protein (g)	4.9	4.8	4.9	4.5	4.5	5.0
Fat (g)	0.2	5.2	6.9	8.6	8.2	5.0
Calories (kcal)	21	66	75	95	92	65
Calcium (mg)	5	9	2	2	2	3
Iron (mg)	0.1	0.2	0.5	0.4	0.2	0.2
Vitamin A (ug)	0	13	0	0	0	0
Vitamin D (ug)	0	6.4	0	0	0	0
Thiamine (mg)	0.02	0	0.01	0.02	0.17	0.02
Riboflavin (mg)	0.02	0.05	0.05	0.05	0.05	0.04
Nicotinic acid (mg)	1.4	2	2.1	2.1	2	2.6

Ministry of Agriculture Fisheries & Food Manual of Nutrition

Cod Kebabs with Barbecue Sauce (page 157) and
Herrings in Oatmeal (page 144)

Buying Seafood

BUYING FRESH FISH

Look for bright eyes, glistening skin and firm flesh. The smell should be pleasingly of the sea – a fresh, salty, brisk and somehow 'right' kind of smell. Reject dullness, red sunken eyes, limp flesh that retains the imprint of your finger, and a smell that is decidedly whiffy. Furthermore, the gills (if present) should be bright blood red, and the scales (if present) should be firmly attached. With fillets, the flesh should be even, firm and springy with no discoloration, dents, or slime.

Some people consider that certain fish – game fish such as salmon, and grey mullet – improve in flavour if kept intact for up to three days from purchase; and that Dover sole has a better flavour after two or three days. This is a matter of opinion and personal taste. One perk of buying a whole fresh fish, ungutted, is that you may find a nice fresh roe (the roe of grey mullet is used for the true taramasalata) – and some fish, like red mullet, are improved by cooking with the liver still in place. If your fishmonger prepares fillets for you, always ask for the head, tail and trimmings for your stock pan.

When buying, remember that most fish are wild sea food. The quality, quantities available and price may be affected by natural conditions – such as the weather, fishing waters or season of the year, when different fish are in prime condition.

Bearing these points in mind, buying fresh fish is very simple. I particularly like shopping for seafood. It can be a proper adventure – the unpredictability of what you are likely to find in any one day on your fishmonger's slab is a real challenge. We can buy so much of our food all the year round – but fish has the unique excitement of a 'real' food, presenting itself to you when it is good and ready. You may have set off to buy a piece of halibut, or a couple of mackerel, and yet you find yourself returning home with a couple of pieces of hake! Your whole day's plan for food is turned upside down, and yet you will have the freshest and most delectable dish on your table by supper time.

Whatever fish is, or is not, available, with the present advanced and sophisticated methods of storage and distribution, you should have no trouble in finding fresh fish, whether at traditional and established fishmongers, market stalls, the travelling fishmonger with his van, or in the increasing number of wet-fish counters in supermarkets.

But do persist in asking for lesser-known species of fish, and do not be put off by remarks like, 'There's no demand for mussels', or, 'All monkfish goes to restaurants', and 'No-one ever asks for John Dory'. *You* can create the demand.

Also, another important point is to experiment with less familiar species of fish whenever possible. On the Isles of Scilly, where I live, I have seen visitors' eyes light up with excitement and curiosity when they see a mixed catch of fish being landed. So few aspiring cooks have the opportunity to try unfamiliar species of fish as they are not always readily available, or they may be uncertain how to tackle the more unusual species, yet there are only a few basic principles to be observed for the cooking of any seafood, and the unusual varieties are well worth trying because many are quite delicious.

It is a shame that our fishermen throw back the spider crab which is considered a delicacy in France. Gurnard, coley, horse mackerel, ling, shad and snapper are often dismissed as inferior – but in the past so too were salmon and oysters which were once food only for the poor. So do persevere – we see too little of so many unusual species of fish because of the apathy of the shopper and lack of imagination of the fish sellers.

Always remember that fishmongers will clean, fillet and prepare any fish to your liking. Most will be happy to advise you on good buys, and cooking methods. However, as this book intends to be a practical guide to all sorts of fish, be adventurous with purchases and refer to the index at the end of the book for recipe ideas.

BUYING SHELLFISH

If you are buying cooked shellfish look for the following points:

The shells of cooked shellfish, such as crab and lobster, should be intact: if they are cracked, the flavour and texture of the meat may have been damaged by water during cooking. Cooked shellfish should feel heavy for their size. You soon develop an instinct for selecting a heavy specimen – it just 'feels' good. Cooked shellfish which feel light for their size, or which have soft shells, may have moulted recently and will be in poor condition. Poor quality lobster or crab will contain liquid if the shells are cracked prior to cooking – test by shaking them gently. Freshly-cooked prawns and shrimps should be firm to the touch and they should be chilled.

In my view, it is well worth the effort of picking out the meat of shellfish in your own kitchen – in particular crab. A dressed crab is slightly more expensive to buy and yet once you have tackled the technique of shelling and extracting meat from your first crab it is a skill that is never forgotten and which improves with practice. Instructions for cooking live shellfish are given on page 32.

BUYING LIVE SHELLFISH

Many people decide that buying and cooking live shellfish or crustaceans is not for them! If that is the case your fishmonger will always have cooked lobsters or crabs for you to buy. If, however, you would like to try your hand at it here are some guidelines to follow.

Make sure your fishmonger sells live shellfish and crustaceans from a reliable source. Better still, if possible, buy direct from a fish market or port as the catch is landed.

With live lobster or crab check that both the main claws are present and that they are packed and sold in moist and cool conditions, and are reasonably lively. Lobster tails should spring back into place when uncurled. The tail of the hen lobster and female crawfish is slightly broader than the tail of the cock lobster and male crawfish: and the hen has slightly more shell around the tailpiece, which protects her eggs or coral. Some people say that all hen lobsters are left-handed and all cocks are right-handed (one of the pair of main claws is always larger than the other). This is not strictly speaking true, so do not depend on this method of selecting lobster and crawfish. There is no difference in the taste of male or female lobsters – and I think that the best weight, live, is around 675 to 900 g/$1\frac{1}{2}$ to 2 lb for the tenderest and sweetest flesh. Much larger lobsters should be cheaper per kilogramme or pound and are more suitable if you are doing a 'grand' dish with a special kind of sauce.

When selecting crab, bear in mind that the cock crab has bigger main claws than the hen crab, and will therefore yield more white meat. The hen crab usually has smaller claws, but the brown meat (cream) inside the body will be found in greater quantity and quality than the cream of the male crab. You

Fettucine alla Trota (page 144), Prawns with Garlic (page 73) and Spicy Pitta Parcels (page 165)

AVAILABILITY OF FISH

	Jan	Feb	Mar	Apr	May	June	July	Aug	Sept	Oct	Nov	Dec
ROUND WHITE												
Bass	●	●	●					●	●	●	●	●
Cat fish		●	●	●	●	●	●					
Cod	●	●				●	●	●	●	●	●	●
Coley	●	●						●	●	●	●	●
Conger Eel			●	●	●	●	●	●	●	●		
Huss	●	●	●	●	●	●	●	●	●	●	●	●
Grey Mullet	●	●							●	●	●	●
Gurnard	●	●	●	●			●	●	●	●	●	●
Haddock	●	●			●	●	●	●	●	●	●	●
Hake	●	●	●			●	●	●	●	●	●	●
John Dory	●	●	●	●	●	●	●	●	●	●	●	●
Ling	●	●	●	●	●	●	●		●	●	●	●
Pollack	●	●	●	●	●	●	●	●	●	●	●	●
Red Mullet					●	●	●	●	●	●	●	
Sea Bream	●	●				●	●	●	●	●	●	●
Whiting	●	●				●	●	●	●	●	●	●
FLAT WHITE												
Brill	●	●				●	●	●	●	●	●	●
Dab	●	●	●	●	●			●	●	●	●	
Dover Sole	●	●			●	●	●	●	●	●	●	●
Flounder			●	●	●	●	●	●	●	●	●	
Halibut	●	●	●			●	●	●	●	●	●	●
Lemon Sole	●	●	●		●	●	●	●	●	●	●	●
Megrim	●	●	●		●	●	●	●	●	●	●	●
Monkfish	●	●	●	●	●	●	●	●	●	●	●	●
Plaice	●	●			●	●	●	●	●	●	●	●
Skate	●	●			●	●	●	●	●	●	●	●
Turbot	●	●		●	●	●	●	●	●	●	●	●
Witch	●	●	●		●	●	●	●	●	●	●	●
OILY												
Anchovy						●	●	●	●	●	●	●
Brown/Rainbow Trout	●	●	●	●	●	●	●	●	●	●	●	●
Eel	●	●	●	●	●	●	●	●	●	●	●	●
Herring	●	●					●	●	●	●	●	●
Mackerel	●	●	●	●	●	●	●	●	●	●	●	●
Pilchard	●	●		●							●	●
Salmon		●	●	●	●	●	●	●				
Sardine		●	●	●	●	●	●					
Sea Trout			●	●	●	●	●					
Sprat	●	●	●							●	●	●
Tunny	●	●	●	●	●	●	●	●	●	●	●	●
Whitebait		●	●	●	●	●	●					

Cuts and Fillets of Fish

CUTLETS
Cut across middle back with a short section of backbone. Not a complete circle (or oval) in contrast to steaks (see below).

STEAKS
Slice across and through thick part of fish including a short section of backbone. Steaks form an unbroken shape. Steaks from flat fish like halibut are oval and sometimes described as cutlets.

MIDDLE CUT
A general term covering a large cut taken from the middle of a round fish.

FILLET
A flat piece of fish cut parallel to the backbone with head, fins and bones removed. Two fillets may be cut from a round fish and two or four from a flat fish.

CUTLETS

STEAKS

MIDDLE CUT

FILLET

QUANTITIES FROM DIFFERENT TYPES OF FISH

	portions per 450 g/1 lb
Cod, haddock on the bone	3
Halibut on the bone	2
Cod and plaice fillet	4
Whitebait	4
Salmon with head and bone	2–3

*450 g/1 lb lobster yields about 225 g/8 oz of edible meat
*675–900 g/1½–2 lb crab yields about 350 g/12 oz of edible meat

Cooking Methods

The main rules for cooking fish are:
* Never overcook it – remember, the flesh is naturally tender.
* Cook fresh fish as soon as possible after buying it.
* To check whether fish is cooked through, test the flesh at its thickest part by piercing with a skewer or sharp knife. When the fish is cooked the flesh will be completely white all the way through and should ease off the bone if unfilleted.
* Serve hot fish dishes straight away – do not keep them warm – and remember that fish will continue cooking when removed from a direct heat.
* If adding salt to the dish do so after cooking as during cooking salt will draw moisture from the fish and can dry it out slightly.
* Always pre-heat the oven or grill.

I cannot emphasise enough the fact that the flesh of fish is naturally tender, and must never be overcooked or the flesh will dry out and flake. In general, most fish can be cooked in under 10 minutes – it's the original fast food!

COOKING METHODS IN DETAIL

Fish is one food that has been known to man throughout the ages. Basic cooking methods have changed very little, except for the invention of the microwave cooker – and aluminium foil . . . how did we ever manage without it?

Fish Fondue (page 124)

SUITABLE COOKING METHODS FOR FISH

The following chart is a good general guide for suitable methods of cooking fish, which are explained in detail on the following pages of this chapter.

Fish	Poaching	Steaming	Braising	Baking	Shallow Frying	Deep Frying	Grilling
Bass	●	●	●	●	●		●
Brill	●	●	●	●	●	●	●
Catfish	●	●	●	●	●	●	●
Cod	●	●	●	●	●	●	●
Coley	●	●	●	●	●	●	
Conger Eel	●		●	●	●		
Dab			●	●	●	●	●
Flounder	●	●	●	●	●	●	●
Grey Mullet		●	●	●	●		●
Gurnard			●	●	●		●
Haddock	●	●	●	●	●	●	●
Hake	●	●	●	●	●	●	
Halibut	●	●	●	●	●		●
Herring			●	●	●		●
Huss	●		●	●	●	●	
John Dory	●	●	●	●	●	●	
Lemon Sole	●	●	●	●	●	●	●
Ling	●		●	●	●	●	
Mackerel	●		●	●	●		●
Megrim	●	●	●	●		●	
Monkfish	●		●	●	●	●	●
Plaice	●	●	●	●	●	●	●
Pollack	●	●	●	●	●	●	
Redfish		●	●	●			
Red Mullet			●	●	●		●
Sea Bream		●	●	●	●		●
Skate	●		●	●	●	●	
Dover Sole	●	●	●	●	●	●	●
Sprats			●	●	●	●	●
Turbot	●	●	●	●	●		●
Whitebait					●	●	
Whiting	●	●	●	●	●	●	●
Witch	●	●	●	●	●	●	●

POACHING

for light and delicate results

Using a well-flavoured stock (court bouillon), fish stock, milk, wine or cider, this is a gentle way to cook whole white fish and large fillets. (See pages 169–70 for recipes). It is not really suitable for oily varieties of fish, with the exception of salmon.

The technique of poaching is simple but one rule must always be observed – the poaching liquid must NEVER BOIL. It should just quiver and shudder, just short of simmering. A fish kettle is not absolutely essential for whole fish as you can improvise with aluminium foil.

Two tips for poaching large, whole fish: make a generous and loose-fitting parcel of aluminium foil around the fish, pour in the poaching liquid, seal, place on a baking tray and poach in the oven.

Or, cut the fish in half, wrap in muslin or foil and poach, then rejoin the halves on the serving dish – disguise the join afterwards with a garnish or with a sauce.

PERFECT POACHING

1. Place the fish in WARM poaching liquid, which should just cover the fish, and put on a gentle heat. Bring slowly up to barely simmering.
2. Continue to poach for 5 to 8 minutes, depending on the size and thickness of fish. Poach whole fish for approximately 5 minutes per 450 g/1 lb, if the fish is to be served hot.
3. For whole fish or cutlets to be served cold, bring the liquid to barely simmering, let it bubble once or twice then remove from the heat. Let the fish cool in the liquid, transfer with a slotted spoon or fish slice to a serving dish and it will be perfectly cooked.
4. You can incorporate the poaching liquid in an accompanying sauce.

BAKING AND ROASTING

for retaining all the flavour

The advantage of baking whole fish is that, with the addition of seasoning and herbs, the fish will cook beautifully in its own juices. To bake whole fish successfully, uncovered, stuffing is recommended to keep the fish moist, and it is a good idea to baste the fish fairly frequently. You can also wrap the fish in lightly greased aluminium foil, or in a paper parcel (en papillote). With either of these two methods, to help retain and add to the cooking juices, you can marinade the fish before cooking. I like to brush baked fish with a little oil or melted butter, or natural yogurt and spices. Whole fish, or fillets, can be baked on top of a bed of vegetables, such as sliced tomatoes, onions, garlic, mushrooms and chopped celery and slightly moistened with a dash of stock, wine, cider, cream or natural yogurt.

PERFECT BAKING AND ROASTING

1. ALWAYS pre-heat the oven.
2. Do not overcook. Test that the fish is ready by inserting a skewer, or sharp pointed knife, into the thickest part of the fish – the flesh should ease off the bone and be opaque.
3. If not parcelled in foil, baste frequently.
4. Serve with its own cooking juices, or incorporate them in a sauce.

STEAMING

the gentle way to cook fish

Steaming is particularly suitable for fish as it has the great advantage that the fish never comes into contact with the water but cooks gently in its own juices.

The fish can be wrapped in paper or aluminium foil parcels, having first been lightly seasoned and sprinkled with lemon juice or a drop of wine. The parcels of fish (which can be marinated first if you like) can also contain thinly sliced vegetables, such as spring onions and slices of fresh root ginger sprinkled with soy sauce (which is a standard Chinese derivation) or leeks, or freshly chopped green herbs.

A conventional steamer can be used, or the steamer rack in a wok, a Chinese bamboo steamer, or simply place the fish between two plates over a pan of boiling water.

PERFECT STEAMING

1. The fish must never come into contact with the water.

2. Keep the water in the steamer or pan boiling. If you have to add more water, use boiling, not cold, water.

3. Test that the fish is cooked by inserting a skewer or a sharp pointed knife into the fish – the flesh should ease off the bone and be opaque. Try not to overcook the fish.

4. Reserve the juices of the steamed fish to be incorporated in a sauce or simply poured over the fish when served.

GRILLING AND BARBECUING

ideal methods of cooking all fish, especially oily varieties

White fish needs basting while it is cooking under the heat of the grill or over the barbecue. It can be marinated first for extra flavour and to protect its delicate and tender flesh. The skin of oily fish will protect the fish better and retain the moisture of the flesh. Remember to oil the grilling rack lightly. Sardines and small herring or mackerel can be grilled very quickly just as they are, but with large, whole fish it is a good idea to make two or three slashes along the back of the fish to allow the heat to penetrate.

Sizzling fish, cooking over the barbecue, produces the most wonderful aroma and is one of my favourite ways of cooking. The same rules for grilling apply to barbecuing, bearing in mind that you must wait for the charcoal to be hot, and burned to a grey colour or, if using wood, wait for the flames to die down to glowing embers. Aromatic herbs can be thrown on the fire to enhance the flavour of the food. Fish can also be parcelled in aluminium foil and barbecued over the fire or pushed into the embers.

When grilling or barbecuing fish kebabs, oil the skewers first to prevent the flesh from sticking to them, and turn the skewers slowly for even cooking, basting all the time.

Mackerel with Tomato and Cucumber Sauce
(page 100)

PERFECT GRILLING AND BARBECUING

1. Always pre-heat the grill, or light the barbecue in advance.
2. Fish should be grilled about 10 cm/4 in above or below the heat.
3. When grilling white fish, baste or brush frequently to prevent the flesh drying out. Melted butter, oil or an oil-based marinade can be used for basting.
4. Grill fish at the last moment and serve straight away.

BRAISING

the all-in-one method of cooking

Braising is a method of cooking fish which falls between baking and stewing, and where the flavour of the vegetables absorbs the flavour of the fish – and vice versa. Braising produces gently cooked and rather comforting fish dishes, and the vegetables, herbs and braising liquid can be served as part of the final dish. A combination of different fish is ideal for this method of cooking – you could try mixing smoked and white fish together, for instance – or taking advantage of best buys and special offers at your fishmonger's. Left-overs from a braise can be used to make soups, or sauces for pasta.

The thick chunks of fish steaks should be placed on top of a mixture of sliced vegetables, herbs and seasoning with water, wine or stock added. The dish should then be covered and baked in a moderate to moderately hot oven or simmered on top of the oven. Either potatoes or noodles can be served with a braise.

PERFECT BRAISING

1. The lid of the cooking dish should fit tightly to prevent evaporation – or you could use a double thickness of aluminium foil.
2. The dish must be cooked slowly to allow the exchange of flavours.
3. Serve all the vegetables and juices from the pan with the fish – or use the juices to flavour accompanying sauces.

FRYING

sautéeing or shallow frying, stir-frying and deep frying

Frying is probably the most traditional British way of cooking fish. In recent years there has been concern that deep frying is not a very healthy method of cooking. However, if done properly, very little fat is absorbed while deep frying as long as the fat is at the right temperature. The blanket term of frying does include some of the quickest and most delicious ways to cook fish, if the basic science of the method is understood and certain rules are followed.

Stir-frying is a good example of a brisk and healthy way to cook fish. You do not necessarily need a wok – although the even heat distribution in the shape of the shallow bowl is ideal for quick cooking – a large, shallow heavy frying pan will do. This method is suitable only for small pieces of fish, and you can stir-fry strips or chunks of fish (such as monkfish) or shellfish (such as prawns, scallops or squid) with a combination of finely chopped vegetables. One of the most important ingredients for successful stir-frying is a good quality oil, such as sunflower or safflower – avoid lard. Preparation for stir-frying must be done before you heat the wok or pan because it is a very quick cooking method. Stir-fry a small quantity of fish at a time, keeping it warm on a plate covered with absorbent kitchen paper to drain off any excess oil. The hot oil immediately seals in the moistness and flavour of the fish and, as soon as the batches of frying are completed, the fish should be served at once.

To sauté or shallow fry is similar in theory to stir-frying. It is best done in a mixture of butter and oil, as the oil prevents the butter from burning. The fish should be dried before cooking or its dampness will cause a layer of steam which will prevent the fish from browning. The pieces of fish can be first dipped in milk or beaten egg and rolled lightly in seasoned flour or fresh breadcrumbs.

To sauté small pieces of fish, as with stir-frying, sauté just a few pieces of fish at a time – transferring them to a plate with a double piece of absorbent kitchen paper on it to absorb any remaining cooking fat. Shake the pan around all the time while cooking so that the fish literally jumps around in the hot oil and butter.

To shallow fry fillets or steaks of fish, coat the fish with a dusting of seasoned flour or egg and breadcrumbs to protect the fish and seal in the flavour. The pan and fat must be hot before the fish is added then, when the fish is browned, reduce the heat and continue frying until tender.

Deep frying in a grease-encrusted deep frying pan of well-used fat is bad news – the eternal 'chip pan' syndrome! Fish coated in batter should be deep fried in good, hot, clean oil. Recipes that spring to mind are goujons (strips of fish in batter) or the Japanese tempura – although, as with Fritto Misto (a combination of batter-coated shellfish and other small chunks of seafood), many of these recipes can, in fact, be shallow fried.

For deep frying, the oil must be brought to the correct temperature (when it is shimmering with heat drop a cube of bread in – it should float straight to the surface and brown immediately). The ideal temperature is 190 c/375 f. When you deep fry fish at the correct temperature, a crust forms on the outside immediately so that hardly any oil is absorbed, and the moisture of the tender flesh is retained.

PERFECT FRYING

1. Always use good quality clean oil, for frying and stir-frying, or a mixture of oil and butter for sautéeing.

Oil used for frying fish can be cooled and strained then stored in a screw-top jar for using again, but discard it when it becomes brown and well used.

2. All fish (or shellfish) needs a protective coating of flour, breadcrumbs or batter before being deep fried.

3. Drain fried food well on absorbent kitchen paper, and serve immediately.

4. In general, fried fish should not be served with rich sauces – wedges of lemon or a sharp tangy dressing are the most suitable accompaniments.

5. One important point to remember is that frying, especially deep frying, is a potentially dangerous method of cooking. Do not over-fill pans with hot oil, and whilst cooking do not leave the frying pan unattended.

Simple Sardines (page 64), Tangy Fish Salad (page 137) and Coley Aubergines (page 92)

MICROWAVE COOKING

A definite advantage of cooking fish in the microwave is that, because there is little or no contact with water and the process of cooking is very quick, the vitamin, mineral and protein content of seafood is retained. The microwave is also invaluable for quick de-frosting and re-heating of cooked fish dishes.

Remember though, as with cooking with gas, electricity and solid fuel, that you must adapt the cooking times to the particular model of microwave oven that you own. The timer control is most important as micro-wave cooking is judged by *time* – not by *time* and *temperature* as in conventional cooking.

Many of the basic cooking rules and methods apply when using the microwave oven, and cooking times and power levels will be given in your particular microwave's instruction book.

The cooking of fish in a microwave cooker is based loosely along the lines of poaching, steaming and baking, but bear in mind the following points. Moisture can affect cooking times as the microwaves react mainly to water molecules. You will have to adjust the liquid used for good results, but always cook fish for the minimum recommended times to avoid overcooking, remembering that fish con-tinues to cook after its removal from the oven. Always cook the fish in a non-metallic container, casserole dish, or oven-to-table ware and avoid dishes which have gold or silver patterns or rims.

Fish can be shallow fried in a microwave oven by using a browning dish – but *deep frying* is not possible as it is extremely difficult to control the temperature of the oil.

When cooking whole fish in the micro-wave, for example herring or plaice, lightly score the skin at the thickest parts to allow the steam to escape and wrap a *small* piece of aluminium foil around the tail portion to prevent it from overcooking. When cooking fish fillets in the microwave tuck under the thin tail end to prevent overcooking.

SMOKING FISH

If you are a keen cook, a keen fisherman, or simply a fish lover, I do recommend you try your hand at home smoking. For this, you need either to buy a home smoker – they are neat and compact, and available from good kitchen shops – or to improvise with large biscuit tins or whatever; but do try it out in the garden for the sake of safety!

The taste of your own freshly smoked mackerel or trout is simply marvellous. An advantage of home smoking is that, after experimenting, you can cook a light, medium or heavy smoked fish. You can brine the fish first, for extra flavour, and of course most smoked fish will keep for up to two weeks.

A home smoker will come with an in-struction book – which usually includes a recipe section. All types of fish and shellfish can be smoked.

COOKING LIVE SHELLFISH

In my view the kindest and most humane way to cook a lobster, crawfish or crab is to plunge it headfirst into boiling water, although I believe the R.S.P.C.A. recommend starting the lobster in cold water and bringing it slowly to the boil, so that it becomes drowsy and then slowly unconscious.

Lobster, crawfish or crab must be boiled in very salty water – about 175 g/6 oz salt to 1.75 litres/3 pints water. You can add a little white wine, vinegar, a bay leaf and bouquet garni if you wish. In general, 10 minutes per 450 g/1 lb is the recommended cooking time, but I find if you boil *any* lobster for more than 30 minutes the flesh becomes rather tough.

Crabs of all sizes can be boiled for 10 to 12 minutes only, and in my experience this unfailingly produces perfect results. Re-member that it is slightly easier to extract the flesh whilst the shellfish is still warm.

COOKING KIPPERS

One time-honoured method of cooking kippers that must be mentioned is to jug them. Simply stand the kippers, tail up, in a heatproof jug and pour boiling water into the jug to completely cover. Leave for about 5 minutes then lift them out by the tail – they will be perfectly cooked, and one advantage of this quick and easy method is that there are no cooking smells!

COOKING SALT COD

Salt cod, or other dried and salted fish such as hake, coley, whiting or ling, should be soaked in several changes of cold water for at least 48 hours. This will plump the fish up to its original white colour. After soaking cut the cod into pieces and simmer in fresh water for 8 to 10 minutes. Alternatively, slice the salt cod into very thin slices, as for Sashimi (see page 65), and serve with finely shredded raw vegetables, soy sauce, grated fresh root ginger and horseradish.

COOKING TIMES

For whole fish, steaks or fillets, and for baking, grilling, poaching or frying, lay the fish on a flat surface and then measure it with a ruler at its thickest point. For each 2.5 cm/1 in of depth allow 10 minutes of cooking time. This method does not apply for soups or stews where, in general, 3 to 8 minutes is sufficient cooking time for bite-sized pieces of fish.

When cooking frozen fish straight from the freezer, just double the cooking time according to the thickness of the fish.

	Poaching	Steaming	Braising	Baking	Shallow Frying	Deep Frying	Grilling
Cod Steak	6–8	15	18–20	15	8–10	—	10–12
Coley Fillet	6–8	15	18–20	15	10–12	4–6	10–12
Haddock Fillet	6–8	15	18–20	15	8–10	4–6	8–10
Herring	8–10	—	18–20	15	8–10	—	6–8
Lemon Sole Fillet	4–5	8–10	10–12	10–12	4–5	3–4	4–5
Mackerel	8–10	—	18–20	15–20	10	—	6–8
Plaice Fillet	4–5	8–10	10–12	10–12	4–5	3–4	4–6
Whiting Fillet	6–8	15	18–20	15	8–10	4–6	8–10

The cooking times are based on 350 g/12 oz boned mackerel, 225 g/8 oz boned herring or cod steak, and 200 g/7 oz of coley, haddock, lemon sole, plaice or whiting fillets.

Freezing Seafood

FREEZING FISH

Freezing is a most efficient way of storing fresh fish (and I mean *really fresh* fish). Unlike other methods of preserving – curing, smoking, pickling or drying – the taste and texture of the fish, when thawed, is practically unaltered. Freezers are also useful for storing many cooked fish dishes. For instance, making double the quantity of fish cakes is hardly any trouble when you are in the mood for a cooking session – and these are perfect for freezing for future use. Another advantage of freezing is that you can freeze dishes made from left-overs of fish, such as mousses, flans, soups, stocks, kedgeree and croquettes. Stock can be frozen in ice-cube trays and used when a tablespoon or two is needed for use in a sauce.

You can cook fish dishes in advance for parties or special suppers and freeze them. Depending on the type of recipe these can be reheated direct from the freezer.

But for me, the freezer is most useful for freezing *fresh* fish – and what could be a more naturally convenient food?

FREEZING FRESH FISH

Whole fish can be frozen intact. If you prefer, you could clean the fish first but in that case stuff the belly cavity with aluminium foil to help keep the shape of the fish. In both cases I prefer to scale the fish first. Remember to use

A typical fishmonger's shop showing a colourful display of fish and shellfish.

the fast-freeze facility if it is featured on your freezer as the quicker the fish is frozen the better the result.

I do not normally give the fish any special pre-freezing treatment, other than wiping clean with a damp cloth or absorbent kitchen paper before wrapping in aluminium foil, freezer cling film or a freezer bag.

Whole fish can also be cleaned and cut into steaks, cutlets or fillets, and frozen individually or in small batches.

PERFECT FREEZING OF FISH

1. Make sure the fish is really freshly caught and choose fish which is at its best for the time of year.

2. Look for species of fish which are in plentiful and low-priced supply.

3. To avoid odours or cross-contamination, take care with wrapping the fish.

4. Freezing any fish which has been previously frozen is not recommended, so consult your fishmonger when buying fish for the freezer.

5. Always label fish with the freezing date.

6. Do not thaw fish in water. It makes the fish soggy, difficult to cook and unappetising.

As a general guide, the maximum storage times for fish are:

White fish	4 months
Oily fish	3 months
Cooked fish dishes	2 months
Smoked fish	3 months

FREEZING COOKED SHELLFISH

Any shellfish you freeze must be very fresh – it should be cooked within 12 hours of being caught, and frozen immediately. Lobster, crawfish and Dublin Bay prawns can be frozen complete in their shell, or you can extract the meat first.

The meat from crab can be picked out and packed in small plastic tubs with lids, wrapped and frozen. Mussels can be cooked first (see page 56) and frozen with their cooking liquid. Clams and oysters should preferably be cooked before freezing. Prawns and shrimps can be peeled or left in their shells. The maximum storage period for all shellfish is 2 months.

PERFECT THAWING

1. Thawing should be timed carefully so that the fish is ready just when it is needed. Place the fish or shellfish on a tray and allow it to thaw in a refrigerator or cool place.

2. Fish can be thawed in a microwave oven.

3. Some fish and cooked fish dishes can be cooked straight from the freezer.

Cooking Utensils

A great deal is made of cooking utensils for certain foods but you honestly do not need anything very special or out of the ordinary for cooking fish, in my view. The basic items to be found in an average kitchen are perfectly suitable. If you were going to be poaching a whole salmon once a week for the next five years I might insist that you invest in a fish kettle, but otherwise you can improvise with aluminium foil. For steaming, two plates over a pan of boiling water are quite satisfactory, rather than buying a special steamer.

However, there are a few small but important items of equipment which are very useful: the most important being good sharp kitchen knives for filleting and preparing fish. A filleting knife should have a long, flexible blade in order to ease it around the bones and flesh of the fish; a heavier and more solid knife is essential for cutting steaks and cutlets of large fish.

Scaling can be done with the blunt edge of a strong knife, although you can buy an inexpensive and effective scaling tool for this job.

For shellfish such as lobster and crab the cracking of shells can be done with a wooden rolling pin, or small mallet. An ordinary hammer could be used but in my experience this tends to shatter rather than crack the shell. The picking out of meat from shellfish can be done efficiently with skewers and both the spoon and handle end of a teaspoon.

Proper oyster knives, however, are cheap and tailor-made for a rather special job – they are also good for scallops, and I would recommend buying one.

For barbecuing and grilling, a pastry brush for basting is a good idea, and a selection of fish slices – at least two – for lifting out whole fish, perforated spoons, tongs and spatulas are essential basic cooking utensils, along with wooden spoons and whisks for sauces, and kitchen scissors for trimming fins from whole fish or cutlets and steaks and cutting through the backbone of fish when boning out (see pages 45 and 47).

All the usual kitchen paraphernalia of casseroles, frying pans, gratin dishes, saucepans and colanders can be used for fish cookery. I have one personal rule (as one who frequently cooks fish) – I keep one large and rather senior saucepan for fish stock, and fish stock alone.

For boiling large lobster, or two or three crabs at a time, you could improvise with a large enamelled washing up bowl or a jam or preserving pan.

A food processor or liquidiser takes away much of the work of chopping and grating, and is marvellous for quick pâtés, mousses, stuffings and sauces. Although some cooks (like me) still relish the occasional enjoyment of using a wooden spoon and bowl, or a pestle and mortar, this is a purely personal preference.

Herbs and Spices

When you read in the recipes in this book, a 'pinch of' or a 'dash of', or 'about 1 tablespoon chopped whatever' – this is for a very good reason. Not only will you have your own personal feelings about a particular herb, spice or flavouring, but with fresh herbs, and freshly ground spices, there will be a variance of strength or flavour, according to the specific variety of any one herb – the size of the leaf and even if the sun was shining when it was picked. One good example is basil, the flavour of which varies considerably according to the variety of plant, and region in which it was grown.

There is also a distinct difference in the flavour of true French tarragon and another variety commonly found which looks similar but has hardly any taste at all.

The most important thing to remember is that the chosen herbs and spices should not overpower the fish – rather they should give the fish in question a gentle nudge in a subtle and flavoursome direction.

For maximum flavour keep dried herbs in their screw-top jars in a cool, dry cupboard. Those attractive herb and spice racks do not always provide the best conditions for storing herbs. Those pretty bunches of herbs dangling down over picturesque farmhouse-style kitchens are also undesirable as they soon lose their flavour and become dusty and grimy.

There are many excellent brands of dried herbs which will give delicious results when used in fish cookery, but do remember to throw out old jars of herbs that have been ornamental or lying around for a long time.

The same applies to ready-ground spices, the flavour of which will deteriorate over a period of time. Best of all, grind or crush whole spices when needed for sauces, dressings or marinades.

HERBS AND SPICES OFTEN USED IN FISH COOKERY

ANISE – or aniseed – is not to be confused with star anise which is a different plant. It is a sort of cross between a herb and spice and should be used in discreet amounts for those who have a definite liking for its distinctive flavour.

BASIL – provides a beautiful smell and lingering taste. It is good with white or oily fish and for soups, sauces and pasta.

BAY LEAF – is used in a traditional bouquet garni. Bay leaves are both decorative and flavoursome for whole baked fish or kebabs.

CARDAMOM SEEDS – one of the ingredients of authentic curry powder. I like to crush a few of these seeds in some marinades.

CAYENNE – is a quite fierce pepper. Use with care in sauces and dressings.

CHERVIL – a delicately flavoured herb which looks rather like parsley. It is suitable with white fish, lovely in sauces and makes an attractive garnish.

CHILLIES – or bottled chilli sauce can be incorporated in small amounts into barbecue sauces, with caution!

CHIVES – a member of the onion family with a milder flavour than the rest. Snipped chives are a common garnish.

A wet-fish counter from a supermarket.

CORIANDER – the fresh leaves are now widely available from supermarkets, delicatessens or Indian shops. Use them or the crushed or ground seeds for a spicy flavour.

DILL – fresh dill is essential for Gravad Lax (see page 64). It also comes in a dried form. The seeds are used for pickled cucumber. Use the chopped sprigs to flavour sauces and salads. It is an annual plant, like basil, and not always easy to find in food or vegetable shops but it it easy to grow from seed.

FENNEL – use the chopped feathery leaves in sauces and dressings for fish, or sprigs for garnish, or the bruised and cracked branches of wild fennel for flavouring and scenting a whole baked fish. The seeds, which look rather like anise seeds, can also be used with discretion in dressings and flavourings.

GARLIC – generally a hint will do for this popular flavouring. It is good for sauces and soups, but be bold with it when making aioli (see page 183).

GINGER – fresh root ginger has to be peeled before being very finely sliced or grated to flavour such dishes as Chinese-style stir-fried dishes. Powdered ginger is totally different and used mainly for cakes and biscuits.

MACE – comes in the form of a 'blade' or ground. It has a strong, sweet, slightly bitter flavour, very similar to nutmeg (to which it is related) but perhaps more subtle.

MARJORAM – fresh or dried, is a favourite of mine and especially good for oily fish.

MINT – I always think of spring or summer when I use mint. It is, of course, traditionally associated with lamb but it is also good with fish and can provide a hint of freshness in some fish salads.

MUSTARD – prepared mustard sauce, or the crushed and sautéed seeds, are classic accompaniments to oily fish.

NUTMEG – a sprinkling of freshly grated netmeg in béchamel-based sauces or in simple fish pies often gives a necessary and subtle flavour to an otherwise bland dish.

PAPRIKA – often confused with cayenne, is in fact a milder form of pepper. For fish cookery it is best for a flourish or as an afterthought garnish to provide colour and effect.

PARSLEY – is probably the most commonly used herb. It has a very good flavour, is marvellous as a garnish, as well as being an excellent source of iron.

PEPPERCORNS – black or white, freshly ground or ready ground. The most commonly used condiment.

ROSEMARY – fresh or dried, this is particularly good with oily fish, especially when barbecuing. A whole branch or sprigs can be put in the charcoal embers, under the sizzling fish, for extra flavour.

SAFFRON – is expensive, but the infused stigma is wonderful for sauces and flavourings for fish. Powdered saffron can be used instead. If you are only after a touch of colour, then you could use a pinch of turmeric.

SAGE – is good for using in stuffings for whole baked fish.

SALT – can be overdone so use sparingly and use sea salt for preference. Try substituting a hint of herbs and spices to sharpen up a dish.

TARRAGON – an absolutely classic herb to use with fish, in sauces or dressings and for garnish. Try to use the true French variety.

THYME – is good for oily fish, and especially if combined with lemon. It is a traditional component of a bouquet garni.

Two Special Mentions

Not commonly found on sale but very good with fish are sorrel and samphire. Both rock or marsh samphire are superb accompaniments for fish. Wild sorrel is prolific in some parts of Britain and cultivated sorrel can occasionally be bought in vegetable shops. Its tart and lemony flavour makes a delicious partner for seafood.

A Note on Wines

Wine is a natural accompaniment to good food, especially fish, and there is such a varied selection on sale at wine shops and supermarkets that I think the most agreeable way to find wines to suit your taste and the flavour of the fish is by drinking it! Most people accept the general rule of white wine with fish and red wine with meat, but there are exceptions and personal preferences. For instance, a cold red table wine is excellent with paella, and, of course, Guinness is wonderful with oysters!

For a simple summer fish salad, or starter of fish terrine, you may like a light and fruity white table wine – although for some people if the salad has a vinegar-based dressing, this would kill the taste and fragrance of a good wine. You can, therefore, use lemon juice instead of vinegar in the dressing.

Many good and inexpensive white wines – dry to medium dry – are ideal to serve with fish. Muscadet, Alsace or Moselle are classic wines to serve with fish and shellfish, as are more expensive wines, like the dry flinty taste of Chablis from the Cote d'Or region, the distinctive fragrance and taste of Pouilly-Fuissé from the Macon region, or the sweeter Vouvray from the Loire valley.

Chilled champagne may be served with all fish, and in the summer I like to serve chilled spritzers (white wine and soda or sparkling mineral water) or simple fruit and wine cups with crushed ice.

With certain shellfish, such as lobster, it is wise to avoid spirits like gin or whisky. Spirits are particularly incompatible with oysters and could cause stomach upsets, or even aggravate or trigger an allergic reaction.

I love many of the good, home-made dry fruit wines with fish, but the main thing to remember with whichever wine you choose is to enjoy your fish!

When cooking with wine, bear in mind that the cooking process burns off the alcohol content, but leaves the enhancing flavour of the wine.

Remember too that, as with the aromatic flavourings of herbs and spices, a suggestion of wine should agree with, rather than dominate, the flavour of fish, and a dash of plonk or left-over wine is fine to enliven or lift a fish dish – but when cooking a really superior fish, such as turbot, John Dory or lobster for example, a good quality wine should be used.

HALIBUT

COD

BRILL

DAB

WHITING

HERRING

SPRAT

PLAICE

LEMON SOLE

DOVER SOLE

A Guide to Fish

There are about sixty species of fish and shellfish on sale in Britain; a glossary of fish names with some of their regional variations (for example, coley is also called saithe, coalfish, or blackjacks) can be found on pages 189–90.

The families of fish can most easily be catagorised as belonging to one of the following groups:

1. PELAGIC: Fish which live in large groups or shoals and frequent the middle and surface layers of the seas, such as herring and mackerel. Trawlers catch these fish as they feed upon plankton and the small crustacea and organisms which drift about in the upper layers of the sea.

2. DEMERSAL: These are bottom fish, which live on or near the sea bed, and include cod and all its relations (like haddock and hake) and flat fish such as plaice and turbot.

3. SHELLFISH: In two general groups: *Molluscs* are shellfish with shells or mantles which have no limbs – such as oysters, clams and mussels (which have bivalves) and cockles and winkles, (which have single shells). They are usually collected by hand.

TURBOT

MEGRIM

HAKE

RED GURNARD

WITCH

HUSS

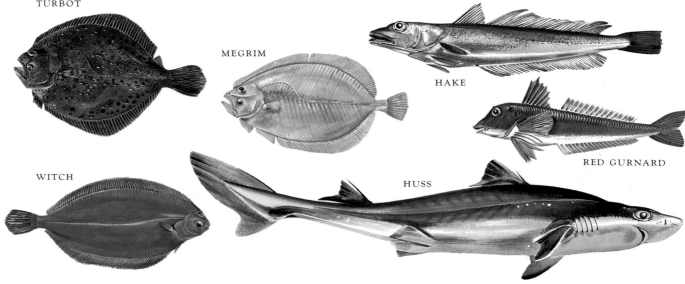

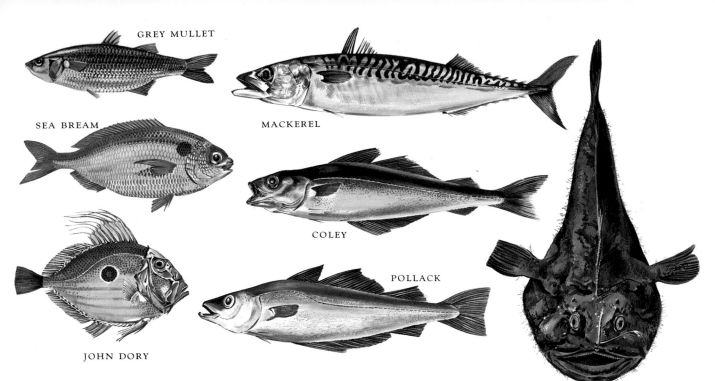

GREY MULLET

MACKEREL

SEA BREAM

COLEY

POLLACK

JOHN DORY

MONKFISH

Crustaceans are shellfish with limbs such as lobsters, crawfish, crayfish, prawns, shrimps or crabs.

QUESTION: When is a prawn not a prawn, but a shrimp? There is always confusion between prawns and shrimps – prawns are slightly larger than shrimps, and shrimps have longer antennae; but they are more or less the same animal, in taste and shape. To add to the confusion, Americans call the British prawns shrimps – and the Dublin Bay prawn is really a type of lobster, also known as scampi or langoustine! *Craw*fish is similar in size and taste to lobster whereas *cray*fish is a smaller freshwater crustacean. One of the fascinations about seafood is that our technological world has not been able to standardise and 'package' the harvest of the sea.

Fish can also be classified in groups of:
a. Round white fish
b. Flat white fish
c. Oily fish
d. Shellfish – crustaceans and molluscs
e. Cartilaginous fish – for example, monkfish, huss and skate.

SKATE

RED MULLET

HADDOCK

LING

SEA BASS

CONGER EEL

Preparing Seafood

SCALING FISH

This is a job which your fish-monger should be happy to do when asked, but is also simple to do at home. Instructions in many fish cookery books fail to point out that it is rather a messy job, and that fish scales do tend to fly around somewhat! So, first cover your work surface with newspaper.

You can buy a fish scaler quite cheaply to do this job, but using the blunt side of a sturdy knife is quite satisfactory.

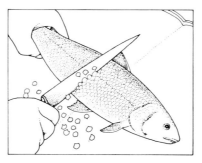

1. Lay the fish on newspaper on your working surface and with the blunt side of a strong knife draw the knife from the tail to the head (i.e. against the flow of the scales).

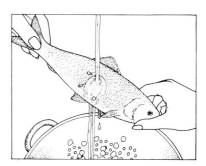

2. Wash the fish under running water, over a colander to catch the scales. Turn the fish on its other side and repeat the process. Wash the fish and pat dry with absorbent kitchen paper. Do not let the scales bung up the sink!

CLEANING FISH

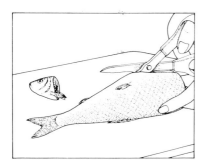

1. Place the fish on its back with the belly facing upwards. Using a sharp knife or scissors cut down the belly and remove the innards.

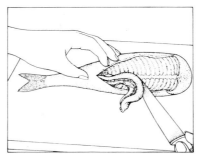

2. If leaving the head on, it is necessary to remove the gills as they will give a slightly bitter taste, otherwise remove the head behind the gills. Wash well.

3. To clean a fish through the gills prise back the gill and, with your other finger and thumb, snap out the gill and pull out the innards all in one go. Wash thoroughly.

FILLETING

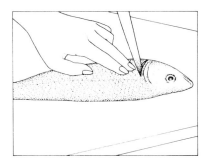 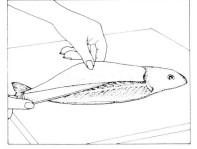 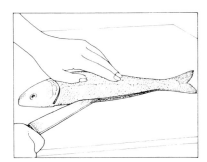

1. Lay the cleaned fish on the chopping board, with its tail and back towards you. Hold the fish steady with one hand and make a semi-circular cut around the head (follow the bone structure and keep close to the head area). Slice along the backbone from head to tail. You should be able to feel the backbone as you keep the knife on top of it while slicing. Beginners can lift the fillet up as they go to see what they are doing.

2. Lift the flesh gently and cut the fillet away from the body, taking care to avoid the 'rib' bones.

3. To remove the lower fillet, turn the fish over and repeat the process. Now you have the two fillets, trim them neatly ready for cooking.

BONING A ROUND FISH

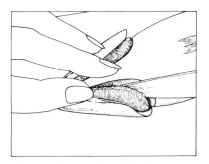 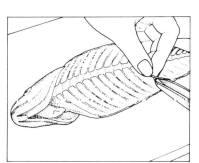 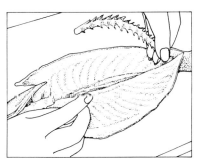

This is the method for boning a whole fish ready for stuffing. Clean the fish as described previously.

1. Remove the gills (these can give a bitter taste when fish are cooked whole). Trim away the dorsal and pectoral fins.

2. Lengthen the opening along the belly and expose the backbone and ribs. You can see the ribs in the flesh of the fish. Work down the backbone of the fish, freeing each rib with the aid of scissors and your fingers. Each rib can then be snapped off the backbone.

3. Now run a sharp knife down each side of the backbone. Using kitchen scissors or game shears, cut through the backbone at the head and pull out the back-bone, working towards the tail where you cut it free.

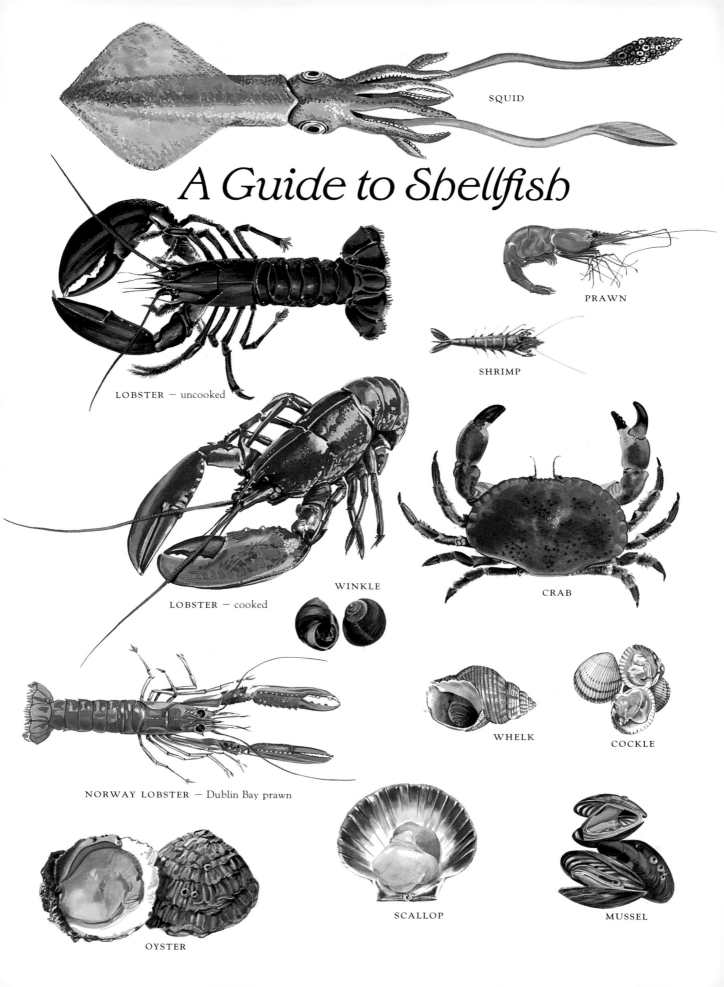

A Guide to Shellfish

SQUID

PRAWN

SHRIMP

LOBSTER — uncooked

WINKLE

LOBSTER — cooked

CRAB

WHELK

COCKLE

NORWAY LOBSTER — Dublin Bay prawn

SCALLOP

MUSSEL

OYSTER

BONING FISH TO PRODUCE BUTTERFLY FILLETS

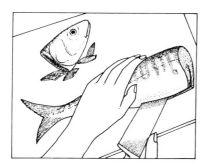

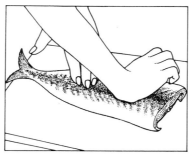

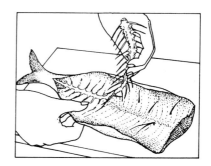

This method is suitable for herring and mackerel, sardines and sprats.

1. Using scissors, cut off the fins. Slice off the head, just behind the gills. Slit the fish along the belly to the tail, and remove the innards – wrap in newspaper and discard.

2. Open the fish and place on a chopping board with the skin uppermost. Using your thumbs or the heel of your hand, press firmly along the centre back of the fish to ease and release the backbone from the flesh.

3. Turn the fish over and ease the backbone away from the flesh, working towards the tail. Any small stray wispy bones still remaining can be removed with tweezers. Wash the fish in cold water and pat dry with absorbent kitchen paper.

FILLETING FLAT FISH

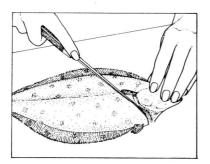

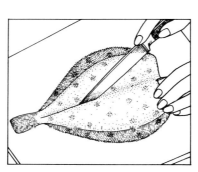

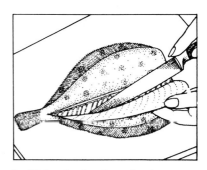

1. Place the fish on a chopping board with the head pointing towards you. To cut the head off, follow the 'shape' of the head with your knife, making sure you leave all the fish and just taking away the bony head.

2. You can feel and see the line of the backbone on the white side of the fish down the centre. Cut a line down the backbone and then insert your filleting knife into the flesh, and feel the tip resting against the backbone and on top of the 'rib' bones.

3. Slide the knife right down the backbone, then work with long, slicing motions across the ribs to the outer edge of the fish. Lift up the fillet, remove, and trim. Repeat on other side – then turn over and remove the other two fillets.

BONING A FLAT FISH FOR STUFFING

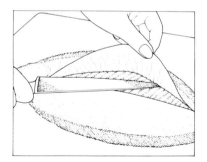

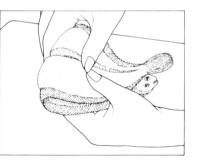

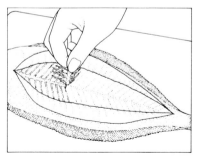

This method (commonly known as pocketing) is good for medium to large fish. It is too fiddly an operation for small-sized flat fish.

1. Leave the head and tail on. Place the fish on a board, dark side up, run your sharp knife down the backbone of the fish and, following the guide on filleting flat fish, gently lift away the fillet on either side of the bone, exposing the ribs.

2. Snap or cut the backbone in several places, either with kitchen scissors or game shears, or by bending back the fish until the bone snaps.

3. Remove these sections of the backbone and ribs with the aid of a small sharp knife. NOTE: The underside skin of the fish and fins are left in place to keep the fish in shape. The fish now has a pouch-type cavity which you can fill with a stuffing.

SKINNING AND BONING MONKFISH

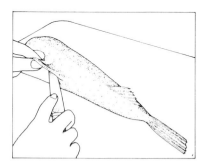

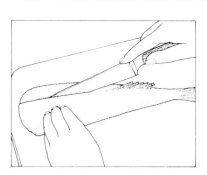

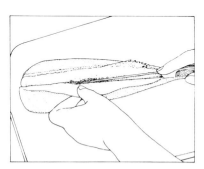

Only the tail end of monkfish is sold commercially.

1. Wash the tail and remove the skin with your fingers and a sharp knife. It will come away easily.

2. With your sharp filleting knife, cut down the centre of the tail to the backbone, from head to tail.

3. Fold back the flesh and cut around the bone and remove. There are no other bones.

SKINNING FISH

Lovers of fish have personal preferences about whether or not, or how, to skin fish. I generally leave the skin on: I think it adds to the flavour of the fish, helps to keep its shape, and looks attractive when served. The speckled orange and brown skin of plaice, with the contrasting yellow of lemon slices, and sprinkling of fresh green herbs melting in tiny knobs of glistening butter is a presentation of the most simple and beautiful kind. However, there are many recipes which call for skinned fish and, of course, your friendly fishmonger will be able to help you out. Large, whole round fish, if they are to be served cold, such as salmon, trout, and grey mullet, can be skinned after cooking, which is a very simple operation. They are then usually garnished with thinly sliced cucumber, radish, capers or sliced olives to choice and/or covered in aspic or aspic mayonnaise. Methods of skinning fresh fish are as follows:

SKINNING FILLETS OF FLAT OR ROUND FISH

When skinning fish fillets, fingers dipped in salt will help you keep a grip on the skin.

1. Place the fillet, skin side down, on a chopping board, tail towards you. Make a 1-cm/½-in snip into the flesh at the tail end, then insert your knife. Holding the tail skin in one hand, work the knife in a sawing action, slicing the flesh away from the skin. Hold the knife at an acute angle (almost parallel) to the fish to avoid cutting the skin. Keep the skin taut, and stop once or twice to fold back the fillet so that you can see how you are going. The skin can be kept for the stock pot.

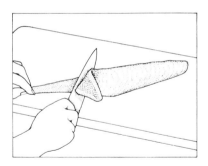

SKINNING A WHOLE FLAT FISH

This is difficult to do, so it is worth attempting only on large fish such as Dover sole. Remember to dip your fingers in salt to get a firm grip. Place the fish, dark side up, on a chopping board. Hold the tail in one hand and, with a sharp knife, cut into the skin at the tail end until you have a good flap to get a grasp on. With a very strong and firm motion, pull the skin towards the head. When you reach the jaws, turn the fish over – hold the fish by the head, and continue pulling the skin until you reach the tail.

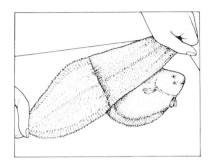

Preparing Shellfish

In French fishing ports and restaurants a crab would be served to you simply cut down the middle of the body, with the claws, and with a wonderful array of salad. Lobster the same – and you would be provided with little instruments like nut crackers, and crochet hooks and long-handled spoons with which to scoop out the edible meat. I think that the average British fish eater prefers the work to be done for him or her. However, do not be frightened of tackling shellfish. It is easy to extract the meat and most rewarding. The freshness of the taste is far superior to frozen or tinned products.

If you are cooking your own crab or lobster you will find it easier to extract the flesh while the shellfish is still warm.

EXTRACTING THE MEAT FROM COOKED LOBSTER OR CRAWFISH

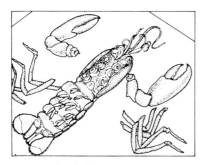 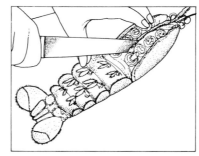 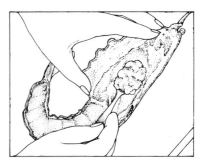

1. Lay the lobster on a chopping board, twist off the main claws and legs and extract the white meat as for the crab on page 52.

2. If you are going to use the halved shells for a cooked lobster dish, or to serve a cold lobster salad, pull back the tail to extend the lobster, lay it on its back and, with a sharp heavy knife, cut down the middle and along the length of the lobster. You may need to give the knife a few sharp taps with a mallet. The white meat is now easily extracted from the tail.

3. With a teaspoon, scoop out the brown meat from the main shell and head. Remember to discard the feathery gills (dead men's or devil's fingers). Remove the easily recognisable sac from the head, and also remove the grey-black thread of intestine running along the tail.

Moules à la Marinière (page 76) and Trout with Almonds (page 117)

EXTRACTING THE MEAT FROM COOKED CRAB

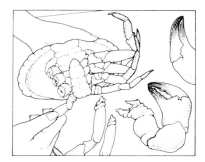

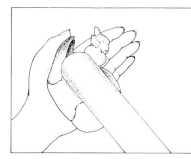

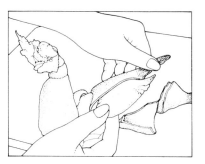

1. Twist off the main claws and legs from the body of the crab: they come away very easily. As the meat is fiddly to extract from the little legs you could instead pound them and boil for stock or soup.

2. To crack the main claws, cup the largest joint in the palm of your hand, and smack it smartly with a wooden rolling pin or mallet. This method should produce a nice clean crack. Hammers or sharp tools, used against a hard surface, will only shatter the shell and give you the extra work of picking out the tiny splinters.

3. Using your fingers, remove the white flesh of the main claws, bearing in mind that there is a flat bone (which feels and looks rather like the end of a miniature plastic spatula) to remove from part of the white claw meat. The handle of a small teaspoon is useful for scooping out the flesh of the two other joints broken off from the main claws.

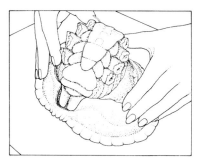

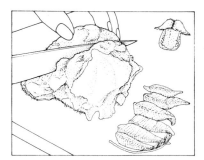

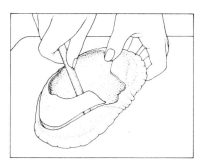

4. Put the body of the crab on a chopping board with the head facing away from you. Push the 'undercarriage' with your thumbs and prise away the underside of the crab so that it comes clean out of the shell. It is very important to remove the soft feathery gills (dead men's or devil's fingers) and the stomach sac (found directly behind the mouth part) as these are not edible.

5. With a heavy sharp knife, cut the underbody in half lengthways and pick out the white meat and creamy brown meat. The brown meat in the shell may be rather watery, so shake out the water and check that the colour of the meat is pink to brown and healthy looking. Scoop out with a teaspoon. For dressed crab, keep the brown meat separate.

6. If the shell is to be used for dressed or devilled crab, tap out the shell inside of the groove around the shell, which is clearly marked, with the tip of a rolling pin or the handle of a wooden spoon. Scrub clean with boiling soapy water before use and do not forget to oil it lightly.

SCALLOPS AND QUEENS

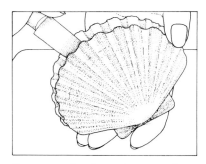

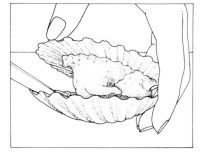

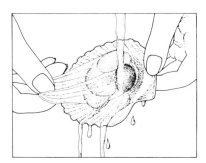

You can also buy these ready prepared in the shell.

1. Opening the shells: This is made easier if you place the shells, hollow side down, on top of a hot cooker, under the grill, or in the oven for a few moments – then they will open slightly. Or you can prise open the shells with a short, stubby, stout knife or oyster knife.

2. Using a longer sharp knife, release the membrance of the scallop from the top and bottom of the shell.

3. Under running cold water, remove the membrane from the white flesh and coral, then trim and clean the scallops on the chopping board. The orange/pink coral and white flesh are the only edible parts. Discard the black intestine. The shells should be well scrubbed and lightly oiled before use.

OPENING OYSTERS

Opening is usually known as 'shucking' an oyster.
I am not pretending that opening oysters is easy for the beginner – but it does get easier as you go along.

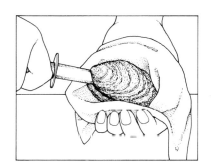

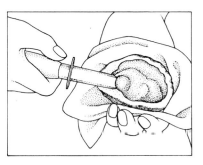

1. Take a tea-towel in one hand to help you take a grip on the oyster. Grasp the oyster firmly, making sure it lies flat side up in your palm. Insert the blade of a short, stout knife (or oyster knife) into the hinge of the oyster and prise open.

2. As you are separating the shells, slide in a sharp knife and cut the oyster free from the top and bottom of the shells. Take care to keep in the juice and remove any flakes of shell that may have fallen on top of the oyster. The oyster is now ready to serve.

Seafood Ring (page 121), Grapefruit and Shellfish Salad (page 140) and Grey Mullet stuffed with Pine Nuts (page 104)

SQUID

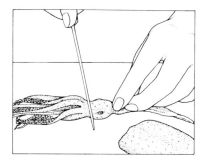 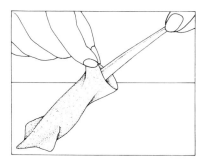 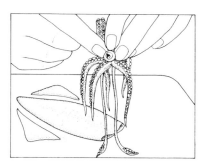

Squid are generally sold prepared for cooking but it is very useful to know how to deal with them should you be presented with this curious-looking cephalopod. Only the tentacles and sac are used for cooking – though sometimes the 'ink' is used for certain dishes. Octopus can be treated in the same way as squid.

1. Pull the head and all of its attachments out of the sac. Cut the tentacles off the head and discard the head and innards attached.

2. Wash the sac under running water, and remove the 'pen' or transparent fin.

3. Pull off the mottled skin of the sac and cut off and reserve the two triangular fins, which are edible. Remove the squid's mouth or beak from the centre of the tentacles. If the squid is to be stuffed, it is now ready. Otherwise, cut the prepared sac into 2-cm/$\frac{3}{4}$-in slices and chop the tentacles in half.

MUSSELS

Mussels have to be absolutely fresh when cooked. Buy the mussels from a reliable source, such as a fishmonger. If you have gathered them yourself, make sure that the area from which you have collected them is unpolluted. Before cooking, place these mussels in clean, salted water and leave overnight. It is important to remember to discard any dead mussels: they must be alive when cooked. Throw away any which do not close when tapped lightly.

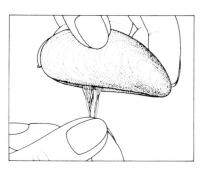

Scrub mussels before cooking. Remove the tuft of hair-like strands from the mussel, known as the 'beard', by pulling away or cutting off with scissors.

COCKLES, WHELKS AND WINKLES

Cockles can be eaten raw, like oysters, or can be boiled in a court bouillon until their shells open. Winkles and whelks should be boiled in water for 5 to 10 minutes for the smaller winkles and 10 to 20 minutes for the larger whelks. A long pin or thin, flexible skewer is indispensable in both cases for extracting the flesh from the shells.

How do you eat it?

This is not meant to be a condescending lecture on how to mind your ps and qs at the table! But, being presented with a whole fish on the bone in a restaurant, or in someone's home, can be a daunting and unnerving first-time experience, bearing in mind that we have been lulled into eating neatly packaged 'convenience' fish, frozen, filleted, ready battered and prepared.

My favourite way of enjoying fish is when it is cooked and served on the bone. It is not difficult to avoid the bones and make a neat job of eating it if you observe the following guidelines.

ROUND FISH

Roll the fish onto its back with your knife and fork. You should be able to see where the backbone is and, holding the fish on the plate with your fork, put your knife on the far side of the backbone and gently push away from you. Move the knife up and down the fish, gently pushing away until the fillet is free from the backbone. Then lay the remaining fillet on the plate, backbone up, ease the knife under the tail and lift gently upwards and towards the head. You may find the fillet reluctant to leave the head – if so, put the knife under the backbone by the neck of the fish, cut down and slide the second fillet away.

Put the backbone and head to one side of the plate or on a side plate, if available.

FLAT FISH ON THE BONE

Cut off the head just behind the gills, severing the backbone. Cut away the fins on each side – these have tasty, crisp flesh on them so do not discard but scrape them down with your fork. Cut down the backbone from head to tail, separate the two fillets and lift them away from the bone. Lift the backbone off the lower fillets and discard.

KIPPERS

A kipper is split open so that when it is served the backbone is exposed. The fillets on one side of the backbone, therefore, are ready to eat. The backbone on the top of the other fillet must be removed. Ease the knife under the tail and pull gently upwards and towards the head. A skilled kipper eater can do this with a knife and fork, but the less skilled can use their fingers – or for that matter ANYONE can use their fingers. Even when you have removed the backbone, and put it to one side of the plate, there are a few large bones near the head of the kipper to watch out for.

Starters

A seafood starter can set the scene for many a memorable meal, moreover there is no reason why you should not continue with a main course of fish as well.

Some starters can be relatively expensive – such as Gravad Lax (see page 64) or Grilled Oysters with Garlic Butter (see page 75) – others can be cheap and cheerful while still being an attractive dish to start a meal – such as Simple Sardines (see page 64) or Soused Mackerel (see page 68). More elaborate, yet not very complicated, starters such as Layered Fish Terrine (see page 60) are enormously satisfying for the creative cook. A simple pâté, on the other hand, can be a great ice-breaker at the start of a supper party, served with crisp tortilla chips or a selection of crudités.

Bear in mind, also, that a great many of the following recipes can be served as main courses by increasing the quantity and serving them with vegetables, salads or pasta.

Scallops with Tangy Orange (page 61) and
Layered Fish Terrine (page 60)

LAYERED FISH TERRINE

Illustrated on page 58

Slices of this terrine are so pretty and impressive that you would think it had taken hours to prepare. In fact it is very simple. The resulting firm texture of this terrine is achieved by careful and accurate cooking, rather than by prolonged preparation. Fennel is not everyone's favourite flavour, so substitute tarragon – or a herb of your choice – if you wish.

about 225 g/8 oz large spinach leaves (or cabbage)
225 g/8 oz firm white fish fillets, chopped
300 ml/$\frac{1}{2}$ pint double cream
3 eggs
1 tablespoon chopped fennel leaves
salt and freshly ground black pepper
225 g/8 oz crab meat
pinch of cayenne
50 g/2 oz pine nuts
a little butter

To serve
1 endive
dill sprigs
tomato rose (optional)

BLANCH the spinach leaves, drain and pat dry. Remove any coarse stalks or ribs then set aside. If you have a food processor or blender, put the chopped fish, cream, eggs, fennel and seasoning into the machine and process until smooth; or finely chop or mince the fish and combine the other ingredients with a fork. Season the crab meat with salt and pepper, add cayenne to taste, then add the pine nuts. Grease a 450 g/1 lb loaf tin or terrine with the butter and carefully line with spinach leaves, leaving enough overlap to fold over the top. Then spoon in half the white fish mixture, and cover with a layer of spinach leaves. Add the crab meat, press down lightly, follow with another layer of spinach, and complete the terrine by adding the remaining white fish mixture.

Fold over the overlapping spinach leaves to cover the top completely and place a sheet of greased greaseproof paper over the terrine. Stand the loaf tin or terrine dish in a baking tin containing 5 cm/2 in boiling water, and bake in a moderate oven (160 c, 325 F, gas 3) for about 45 minutes, or until the loaf is nice and firm to the touch. When it has cooled off slightly, invert the tin and turn out. Cool, then chill for several hours. Carefully slice and serve on a bed of endive with dill sprigs to garnish. You can also make a rose from a tomato, if liked. SERVES 6–8

TARAMASALATA

The true taramasalata is made from the roe of the grey mullet, but smoked cod's roe will do just as well. The lovely taste and texture of home-made taramasalata is far removed from the plastic cartons of some of the commercial varieties.

225 g/8 oz smoked cod's roe
3 or 4 thick slices white bread
2 cloves garlic, crushed
300 ml/$\frac{1}{2}$ pint olive oil
juice of 1 lemon
freshly ground black pepper

REMOVE the skin from the cod's roe and soak in water for 1 hour to lessen the saltiness. Remove the crusts from the bread and soak the bread in cold water. Pound the roe and crushed garlic together. Squeeze out the bread and add to the mixture, continuing to beat. Add the oil a little at a time, beating continuously, until the desired consistency is achieved. Season with the fresh lemon juice and freshly ground black pepper. Chill the taramasalata, and serve with black olives, lemon wedges and toasted bread. Or, instead of bread, you could serve this dip with celery sticks or scrubbed raw carrots. SERVES 4

SEAFOOD PROFITEROLES

Illustrated on page 19

These are very light, and two or three on a plate with small bouquets of watercress and twists of lemon make an attractive starter – they would also be good as part of a buffet lunch table.

2 tablespoons soured cream
1 teaspoon concentrated tomato purée
salt and pepper (optional)
1 fillet hot-smoked mackerel or smoked salmon pieces
cayenne to dust
watercress sprigs and lemon twists to garnish

CHOUX PASTRY
50 g / 2 oz butter
150 ml / $\frac{1}{4}$ pint water
50 g / 2 oz white flour
50 g / 2 oz wholemeal flour
$\frac{1}{4}$ teaspoon cayenne
2 medium–large eggs

FIRST of all make the choux pastry. Put the butter and water in a saucepan and bring up to the boil. Take off the heat and beat the flours and cayenne in straight away until the dough that forms leaves the side of the pan. Let the mixture cool down, then gradually beat in the eggs a little at a time until the dough mixture is thoroughly amalgamated. Place teaspoons of this dough – it should make about 18 choux buns – on a lightly greased baking tray, and bake in a moderately hot oven (200 c, 400 f, gas 6) for about 20 minutes until risen and firm. Transfer to a wire rack to cool.

Meanwhile, combine the soured cream and tomato purée to make a dressing – season lightly if you wish. Skin the mackerel or salmon and flake or cut into small strips. Cut open each choux bun, fill with a little of the dressing, and top with flakes of the fish. Serve on white plates, three to a plate, with a dusting of cayenne and a garnish of watercress sprigs and lemon twists. SERVES 6

SCALLOPS WITH TANGY ORANGE

Illustrated on page 58

For a more substantial dish, serve the scallops on a bed of buttered noodles.

8 scallops
50 g / 2 oz butter
1 bunch spring onions, finely chopped, including green parts
1 clove garlic, finely chopped
juice of 1 orange
salt and freshly ground black pepper
2 teaspoons double cream or crème fraîche
orange twists to garnish

OPEN and prepare the scallops (see page 53). Slice the white flesh. Sauté the white and coral sections of the scallops in the butter for 2 to 3 minutes. Remove the scallops with a slotted spoon, and keep warm. Put the spring onions and garlic into the pan and cook gently until soft. Add the orange juice, salt and pepper and stir well, taking up all the juices. Remove from the heat and swirl in the cream or crème fraîche. Arrange the scallops on individual plates and spoon over the sauce. Garnish with twists of orange. SERVES 4

FISH TARTLETS

Use cod or any other firm white fish (for example, coley or pollack) for these exquisitely flavoured little tartlets.

350 g / 12 oz cod fillet, cooked, skinned, and
sliced into thin pieces
100 g / 4 oz soft goat's cheese
2 egg yolks, beaten
2 tablespoons single cream
2–3 teaspoons chopped fennel leaves

SHORTCRUST PASTRY
100 g / 4 oz wholemeal flour
100 g / 4 oz plain flour
pinch of salt
100 g / 4 oz butter or margarine
2 tablespoons cold water

FIRST make the pastry by sifting together the flours and salt. Rub in the butter or margarine until the mixture resembles fine breadcrumbs. Sprinkle over the water and bind the mixture together. Roll into a ball and chill for 20 to 30 minutes before using.

Roll out the chilled pastry and, using a pastry cutter, stamp out 12 rounds and use to line greased patty or bun tins. Bake blind in a moderately hot oven (200 c, 400 f, gas 6) for 10 to 12 minutes. Cool on a wire rack.

When cooled, put a layer of cod into each tartlet. Combine the goat's cheese with the egg yolks, cream and chopped fennel, and top the fish with a spoonful of this mixture. Bake in a moderately hot oven (200 c, 400 f, gas 6) for a further 10 minutes. Serve hot or cold with a salad garnish. SERVES 4–6

COULIBIAC

450 g/1 lb salmon fillet
100 g/4 oz butter
salt and freshly ground pepper
1 onion, finely chopped
100 g/4 oz rice
175 g/6 oz mushrooms, sliced
1 hard-boiled egg, roughly chopped
grated rind and juice of ½ lemon
1 tablespoon chopped fresh dill
1 tablespoon chopped parsley
*450 g/1 lb flaky or puff pastry, defrosted if
frozen*
1 egg, beaten
300 ml/½ pint soured cream to serve

PLACE the salmon fillet on a large piece of aluminium foil. Melt half the butter and sprinkle over the salmon. Season with a little salt and pepper and wrap the salmon in the aluminium foil. Place in a cool oven (150c, 300f, gas 2) for 25 minutes.

Soften half the onion in half the remaining butter, add the rice and mix thoroughly. Add 450 ml/¾ pint water, simmer for 20 minutes, until the liquid has been absorbed. Allow to cool. Soften the remaining onion in the rest of the butter. Add the mushrooms and cook lightly. Leave the mixture to cool. Skin the salmon and chop the flesh into fairly large chunks. Mix together the rice, onion and mushrooms, salmon, egg, lemon rind and juice, dill and parsley. Season well with salt and pepper.

Roll out half the pastry to a large rectangle of about 30 × 18 cm/12 × 7 in or four small rectangles. Place in the centre of a lightly greased baking tray. Lay the filling on top. Roll out the remaining pastry and place on top. Press the edges together well and brush all over with beaten egg. Place in a hot oven (230c, 450f, gas 8) for 35 to 45 minutes, until the pastry is a rich golden brown. (If the pastry browns too quickly, cover with greaseproof paper.) Serve hot or cold with soured cream. SERVES 6

SIMPLE SARDINES

Illustrated on pages 30–1

12 fresh sardines
225 g/8 oz ricotta cheese
salt and freshly ground black pepper
lemon wedges and brown bread and butter to serve

REMOVE the heads from the sardines. Split down the belly and clean. Turn over and press down the backbone, turn back to skin side down and remove the backbone.

Spread each sardine with a generous amount of ricotta cheese, season to taste and roll up. Grill under a hot grill – or barbecue. Serve immediately with wedges of lemon and brown bread and butter. SERVES 4–6

GRAVAD LAX

Illustrated on pages 66–7

Gravad lax, also known as gravlax, is Scandinavian dill-pickled salmon. It is very expensive to buy but you can make it yourself for a special occasion for no more than the cost of good fillet steak for two. You could also treat mackerel, trout or herring in the same way.

675 g/1½ lb tail piece of salmon or salmon trout
1 large bunch fresh dill
2 teaspoons peppercorns, crushed
2 tablespoons sea salt
1 tablespoon caster sugar or clear honey
1 tablespoon brandy
dill sprigs or flowers to garnish

FIRST scale, bone and fillet the fish (see pages 44–7), or ask your fishmonger to do this for you, but still leaving the skin on. Mix together the remaining ingredients, except for the dill. Place one half of the fish, skin side down, in a flat dish and rub half the curing mixture into the flesh. Top with the bunch of dill. Rub the second fish half with the remaining mixture and place, skin side uppermost, on top of the first salmon half. Cover with aluminium foil or cling film and place a heavily weighted plate or basin on top. Chill for at least 36 hours, turning every 12 hours or so. The pale pink flesh of the salmon will compress and deepen in colour during this time, like that of smoked salmon.

When it is ready to serve, remember that it is very important to carve the fish on the bias for the correct texture and taste. Scrape off the dill and seasonings then, using an extremely sharp knife, slice the salmon into very thin slices. Arrange the slices on a serving dish or on individual plates and garnish with fresh dill sprigs or flowers. Accompany the gravad lax with the following sauce. SERVES 8

MUSTARD AND DILL MAYONNAISE

2 tablespoons Dijon or German mustard
1 tablespoon caster sugar
1 large egg yolk
150 ml/¼ pint olive oil
1 tablespoon finely chopped dill
lemon juice or white wine vinegar to taste

MAKE up the mayonnaise according to the instructions on page 181. Add the dill and a squeeze of lemon juice or dash of white wine vinegar to taste.

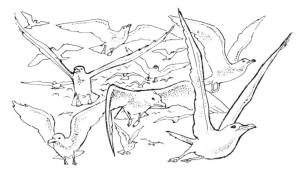

SMOKED TROUT WITH CELERIAC REMOULADE

————— Illustrated on pages 66–7 —————

300 ml/½ pint mayonnaise (page 181)
3 tablespoons natural yogurt
1 tablespoon Dijon mustard
squeeze of lemon juice
salt and freshly ground black pepper
1 large celeriac or 2 heads celery
4 smoked trout, filleted if preferred

TO SERVE
endive leaves
lemon slices
2 black olives

IN a large bowl, beat together the mayonnaise, yogurt and mustard and season with lemon juice, salt and freshly ground black pepper to taste. Shred the celeriac – or cut the celery into matchsticks – and fold into the dressing. Arrange the smoked trout on four plates, and heap a large tablespoon or two of the celeriac mixture on the side of each trout. Serve with the endive, slices of lemon and half a black olive. SERVES 4

SMOKED MACKEREL PÂTÉ

2 whole or 4 fillets hot-smoked mackerel
50 g/2 oz butter, softened
1 clove garlic, crushed (optional)
1 tablespoon lemon juice
freshly ground pepper

REMOVE the skin and any bones from the fish then flake into a bowl. Add the butter and garlic, if using, and mix together thoroughly until well combined. Stir in the lemon juice and seasoning, tasting until desired piquancy is achieved. Serve with squares of Melba toast or hot brown toast. SERVES 4

KIPPER PÂTÉ

225–275 g/8–10 oz cooked kipper fillets
50 g/2 oz butter, softened
juice of 1 lemon
1 tablespoon concentrated tomato purée
freshly ground black pepper

REMOVE the skin from the kipper fillets and place in a food processor or blender. Add the butter, lemon juice, tomato purée and a sprinkling of black pepper. Purée until smooth and well mixed. Turn out into a dish, fork up the top decoratively, then chill thoroughly. Serve with wedges of lemon, crispbread or brown bread and butter. SERVES 4

SASHIMI

————— Illustrated on pages 66–7 —————

Use really fresh fish for this Japanese dish. The idea of raw fish may seem strange for our Western palate – but be bold. It is an exciting recipe and makes a super summer starter. Do try this recipe – it really is *good*!

450 g/1 lb cod fillet, monkfish, sea bream, sea
bass or any firm white fish
2 tablespoons coarsely chopped parsley
1 bunch watercress
1 radiccio
1 tablespoon powdered or freshly grated
horseradish or 3 tablespoons horseradish sauce
3 tablespoons soy sauce

WASH and skin the fillets (see page 49) and pat dry. Slice them into very thin slices or flakes. Arrange them on individual plates, surrounded by the parsley, watercress and radiccio. Combine the horseradish and soy sauce and serve separately as a dip. Use fingers, chopsticks or forks. SERVES 6–8

Smoked Trout with Celeriac Remoulade (above),
Gravad Lax (page 64) and Sashimi (above)

SOUSED MACKEREL

For a fine and elegant taste this white wine vinegar marinade is excellent. You could, however, use a mixture of malt vinegar and water, or beer and water, for a pleasantly earthy result.

4 medium mackerel
1 large onion, sliced
about 12 black peppercorns, crushed
2 bay leaves
150 ml/¼ pint white wine vinegar
150 ml/¼ pint water
lemon wedges and brown bread and butter to serve

Sauce
225 g/8 oz watercress
150 ml/¼ pint soured cream
squeeze of lemon juice
dash of Tabasco sauce
pinch each of salt and freshly ground black pepper

GARNISH
sliced radishes
peeled cucumber matchsticks

CLEAN the mackerel, wash and pat dry with absorbent kitchen paper, then place in a large baking dish.

Sprinkle over the sliced onion, crushed peppercorns and bay leaves. Cover with the combined wine vinegar and water. Bake in a moderate oven (180 c, 350 f, gas 4) for 20 to 25 minutes. Let the fish cool in the liquid then lift them out carefully with a perforated spoon or fish slice. Peel off the skin from the mackerel and discard if wished, or leave the skin on. (It is better to fillet the mackerel after cooking as it is easier to do and the whole flavour of the fish is retained while it is cooking.) Chill the fish.

To make the sauce: purée the watercress in a food processor or blender for a few seconds then add the remaining sauce ingredients. Chill the sauce.

Pour a little sauce onto four plates, place a mackerel fillet on top and garnish with the radish slices and matchsticks of peeled cucumber. Serve with the lemon wedges and brown bread and butter. SERVES 4

ROLL MACS

A lovely starter for which you need a piquant fruit chutney. I use a home-made plum and raisin chutney, sharpened up with a little lemon juice.

4 small to medium mackerel or 8 fillets
1 medium onion
100 g/4 oz button mushrooms
a little butter
2–3 tablespoons white wine
3–4 tablespoons fruit chutney
2–3 tablespoons soured cream

CLEAN the mackerel, and take off the fillets (see pages 44–7), leaving the skins on. Slice the onion and mushrooms thinly and scatter them over the base of a lightly buttered gratin dish. Moisten with a little white wine. Lay the fillets, skin side down, on a board and spread each with a very little chutney. Roll each one up towards the tail end and arrange on the onion and mushroom base, neatly tucking the tails under each roll. Spoon over 2 tablespoons of chutney, covering each roll, and bake in a moderately hot oven (200 c, 400 f, gas 6) for 20 minutes. A nice shiny brown crust will form on the top of each roll.

Put two rolls on each plate, and surround with a spoonful of the mingled wine and chutney liquid and garnish with the mushrooms and onion slices. Put a spoonful of thick soured cream on top of each roll and serve straight away. SERVES 4

SMOKED FISH MOUSSE

———— Illustrated on page 7 ————

*175 g/6 oz smoked trout, salmon or mackerel
fillets
50 g/2 oz fromage blanc or low-fat curd cheese
1 tablespoon lemon juice
pinch each of salt and white pepper
15 g/½ oz powdered gelatine
3 tablespoons hot water
150 ml/¼ pint double cream
1 large egg white
watercress sprigs to garnish
Cold Tomato Sauce to serve (page 177)*

PURÉE the smoked fish in a food processor or blender with the fromage blanc, lemon juice and a little seasoning. Dissolve the gelatine in the hot water and add to the fish mixture. Turn into a bowl and leave in a cool place until it begins to set. Whip the double cream and whisk the egg white until stiff. Stir the fish mixture well then fold in the double cream and whisked egg white. Put into a prepared mould and chill. Turn out onto a chilled plate – surround with sprigs of watercress and pour around a border of cold tomato sauce or serve the sauce separately. SERVES 4

GOUJONS

These are always popular, especially with children, and you can use a selection of firm white fish – look for varieties in plentiful supply. Do all the preparation first and shallow fry at the last moment before serving.

*675 g/1½ lb white fish fillets, skinned (page 49)
1 quantity Light Batter (page 185)
oil for frying
cress and cucumber slices to garnish
lemon wedges and bread to serve*

CUT the fish into thin strips, about 6–7 cm/2½–3 in long by 1 cm/½ in thick, remembering to dry them well with absorbent kitchen paper to achieve better results when frying. Prepare the batter and leave to settle for 30 minutes. Dip the strips in batter and fry in small batches to prevent them sticking. (You could use a wok for this.) Drain the goujons on absorbent kitchen paper and keep warm until all the strips are cooked. Garnish the goujons with cress and butterfly slices of cucumber. Serve immediately with wedges of lemon and fresh bread. SERVES 6

SMOKED HADDOCK CREAMS

These little ramekins make a lovely low-fat starter, served with wholemeal toast and wedges of lemon. The creams can be turned out and set on a platter of watercress and garnished with thin strips of lemon peel and a sprinkle of paprika.

*225 g/8 oz smoked haddock fillet, flaked
1 egg and 1 egg yolk
juice of 1 lemon
100 g/4 oz quark or low-fat curd cheese
100 g/4 oz natural yogurt
dash of Tabasco sauce
pinch each of salt and pepper*

SIMPLY process all the ingredients in a food processor or blender until smooth. Spoon into individual ramekins or small soufflé dishes, stand in a baking tin, pour in boiling water to one-third of the way up the ramekin or soufflé dishes and bake in a cool oven (150 C, 300 F, gas 2) for about 20 minutes. SERVES 4

SMOKED TROUT AND ANISE RAMEKINS

Illustrated opposite

This is so simple to prepare and has an unusual and delicious tang – it is also low in fat. It could also make a satisfying lunch with salad and toasted wholemeal bread.

*275 g / 10 oz smoked trout, filleted and flaked
100 g / 4 oz cottage cheese
100 g / 4 oz fromage blanc or low-fat curd cheese
juice of $\frac{1}{2}$ lemon
1 teaspoon anise, or Pernod or Ricard
pinch each of salt and freshly ground black pepper
brown bread and lemon wedges to serve*

COMBINE all the ingredients in a food processor or blender, or mix by hand for a pleasingly rougher texture. Pile into individual small ramekins or soufflé dishes and chill. Serve with brown bread and wedges of lemon. SERVES 4–6

FRITTO MISTO DI MARE

Illustrated opposite

For me, this brings back memories of sunny holidays in the Mediterranean years ago, which was the first time I had this tempting mixture of crispy seafood.

*about 675 g / 1$\frac{1}{2}$ lb mixed seafood, including squid, sole, scampi and whatever else is available
seasoned flour or Light Batter (page 185) to coat
oil for frying
lemon wedges to serve*

PREPARE the squid (see page 56) or buy it prepared from the fishmonger, slice the sac into 5-mm / $\frac{1}{4}$-in rings and cut the tentacles in half. Cut the sole into strips, and slice the scampi. Make sure all the fish is dried well with absorbent kitchen paper. Put the seasoned flour into a large polythene bag with the fish and shake until all the fish is coated; or coat the fish with the batter. Heat the oil in a frying pan or wok and fry the fish in small batches until crisp and golden brown. Drain each batch on absorbent kitchen paper and keep hot until all the fish is cooked. Serve immediately with lemon wedges. SERVES 6–8

COURGETTES STUFFED WITH CRAB MEAT

This is a very simple starter. The fragile taste of the courgettes contrasts and offsets the richness of the crab.

*4 large courgettes
1 red pepper
350 g / 12 oz crab meat
2 teaspoons double cream
1 tablespoon mayonnaise (page 181)
$\frac{1}{4}$ teaspoon Tabasco sauce
salt and freshly ground black pepper*

CUT the stalks off the courgettes then cook in boiling water for about 8 minutes. Drain, cool and slice in half lengthways. Scoop out the seeds from the middle of the halved courgettes.

Deseed and finely chop the red pepper. Mix together the red pepper, crab meat, cream, mayonnaise, Tabasco and season with salt and pepper to taste. Heap into the middle of the courgettes and bake in a hot oven (220 C, 425 F, gas 7) or under the grill for about 10 to 15 minutes. SERVES 4

Smoked Trout and Anise Ramekins (above) and Fritto Misto di Mare (above)

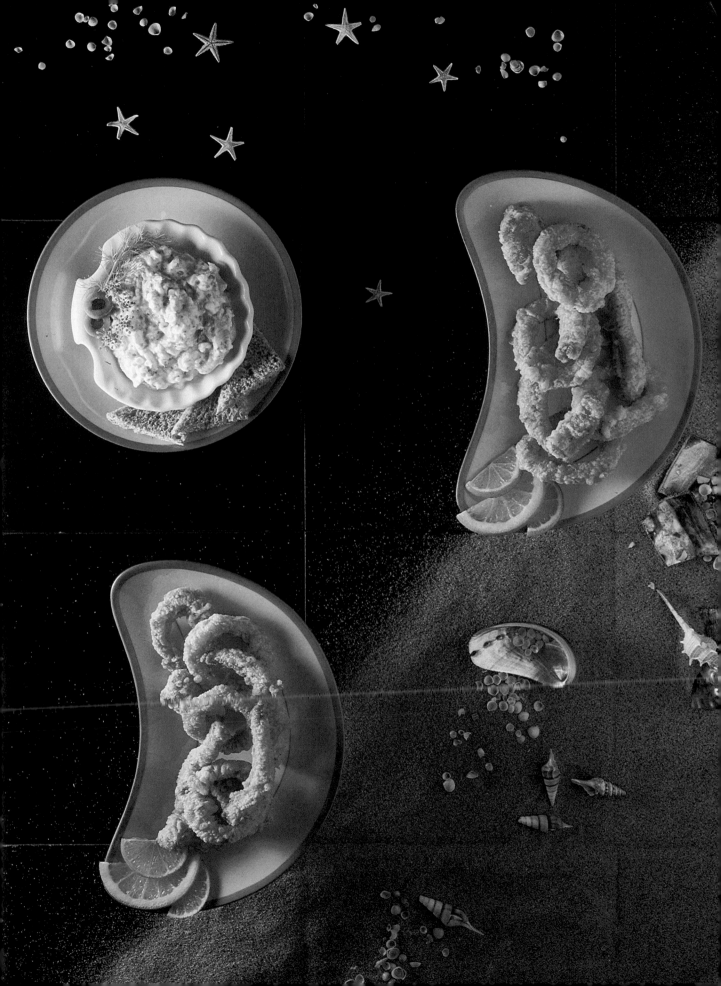

MEGRIM FILLETS WITH CITRUS MARINADE

Illustrated on pages 186–7

You can use other flat fish for this recipe, for example plaice or witch.

*4 medium megrim or 8 fillets
a little olive oil
juice of 1 lime
salt and freshly ground black pepper
chopped parsley and olives to garnish
lime and orange wedges to serve*

MARINADE
*1 large clove garlic, crushed
juice of 1 lime
juice of 1 orange
4 tablespoons olive oil
1 medium onion, finely chopped
a few drops of Tabasco*

SALAD
*crisp lettuce or endive
sliced tomatoes
cucumber*

TAKE the fillets off the megrim (see page 47) or ask the fishmonger to do this for you, brush with olive oil and sprinkle with lime juice, season, and grill for 3 minutes each side, basting all the time.

Combine the marinade ingredients and use to cover the cooked fish. Cover the dish with cling film and refrigerate overnight. Lift out the fillets with a slotted spoon and arrange on a bed of mixed green salad. Pour over a little of the strained marinade and garnish with the parsley and olives. Serve with wedges of lime and/or orange. SERVES 4–6

HERRING SANDWICH

*8 herring fillets
salt and freshly ground black pepper
1 bunch dill, chopped
4 tablespoons horseradish sauce
4 tablespoons soured cream or natural yogurt
sesame seeds
50 g/2 oz unsalted butter
lemon wedges and brown bread and butter to
serve*

MAKE sure there are no fine bones left in the fillets. If there are any, remove with tweezers.

Lay two fillets skin-side down, season well and sprinkle with a quarter of the fresh dill. Generously spread one fillet with 1 table-spoon horseradish sauce and the other with 1 tablespoon soured cream or yogurt. Press together like a sandwich and coat in the sesame seeds. Repeat the process with the remaining fillets. Fry for 4 to 5 minutes on each side in the unsalted butter, and serve with wedges of lemon and brown bread and butter. SERVES 4

PRAWNS WITH GARLIC

———— Illustrated on pages 13–14 ————

50 g/2 oz butter
1 small onion, finely chopped
2 large cloves garlic, crushed
1 small red pepper, deseeded and chopped
450 g/1 lb peeled cooked prawns or sliced
Dublin Bay prawns (scampi)
1 tablespoon lemon juice
salt and freshly ground black pepper
chopped parsley to garnish

IN a heavy frying or sauté pan, melt the butter and gently cook the onion, crushed garlic and pepper until soft but not browned. Turn up the heat slightly, and add the prawns, mix well and sauté for 2 to 3 minutes. If using scampi, cook for 4 to 5 minutes. Add the lemon juice, check the seasoning and garnish with chopped parsley. Serve immediately with a plain crisp green salad and fresh bread to mop up the garlic juices. SERVES 4–6

COQUILLES SAINT JACQUES

8 scallops
300 ml/½ pint milk
salt and pepper
50 g/2 oz butter
50 g/2 oz mushrooms, thinly sliced
25 g/1 oz flour
1 tablespoon dry sherry
50 g/2 oz fresh breadcrumbs
50 g/2 oz Cheshire cheese, grated
½ teaspoon mustard powder
lemon twists and parsley sprigs to garnish

PREPARE the scallops as described on page 53 and slice in half. Gently poach the scallops in the milk seasoned with salt and pepper for about 4 minutes. Drain and reserve the stock.

Melt the butter and sauté the mushrooms for 2 minutes. Stir in the flour and gradually add the reserved stock (made up to 300 ml/½ pint with more milk if necessary). Bring to the boil, stirring continuously. Stir in the scallops and sherry and spoon back into the scallop shells or small dishes.

Mix the breadcrumbs, cheese and mustard powder together and sprinkle over the scallop sauce. Place under a moderate grill until golden brown and bubbling. Garnish with lemon twists and parsley sprigs then serve. SERVES 4

LITTLE FISH RAMEKINS

a little butter
225 g/8 oz hake fillet, skinned
salt and freshly ground black pepper
175 g/6 oz peeled cooked prawns
about 2 tablespoons fish stock (page 170) or
white wine
2 tomatoes, peeled and sliced
175 g/6 oz Gruyère cheese, grated
1 (212-g/7½-oz) packet frozen puff pastry,
defrosted
1 egg, beaten, to glaze

LIGHTLY butter six ramekin dishes. Arrange small pieces of the raw hake in the bottom of each dish and season lightly with the salt and pepper. Top with the prawns and moisten with a little stock or white wine. Cover with 2 or 3 slices of tomato then with the cheese.

Roll out the defrosted pastry on a floured board. Cut out triangles from the pastry and place on top of the ramekins so that the top of the triangle faces down into the mixture in the ramekin and the remaining points are sticking out slightly. This will allow the cheese to bubble up and brown. Brush the pastry with a little beaten egg before baking in a hot oven (220 C, 425 F, gas 7) for 15 to 20 minutes, until the pastry has risen and is golden. Let the ramekins stand for a few minutes before serving. SERVES 6

DRESSED CRAB

Illustrated opposite

Preparing a dressed crab is great fun – there is no mystique about it and the result is pretty and impressive.

2 (675-g / 1½-lb) crabs
salt and freshly ground black pepper
2 hard-boiled eggs
4 tablespoons finely chopped parsley
paprika
a few drops of lemon juice

To Serve *(optional)*
green salad
mayonnaise
lemon wedges
brown bread and butter

EXTRACT the white and brown meat from the crabs as explained on page 52 and keep separate. Reserve any coral you may find. If you have not already picked out the eight little legs of the crab, crack their main joints and reserve for garnish.

Tap out the shell of the crab as described on page 52 then wash thoroughly and dry.

Lightly season the crab meat with salt and pepper. Separate the yolk and white of the hard-boiled eggs and chop finely. Arrange the brown crab meat down the sides of each shell then place a strip of white hard-boiled egg next to them. Make a similar strip of parsley followed by the egg yolk. Heap the white crab meat in the centre of the shells and sprinkle with a little lemon juice. Sprinkle the paprika in a line down beween the egg yolk and the white crab meat or use the reserved coral, if you have any.

Set the dressed crabs on a platter of green salad and arrange the reserved, cracked little crab legs around them in a decorative fashion. Serve with mayonnaise, wedges of lemon and brown bread and butter. SERVES 6–8

Dressed Crab (above) and Grilled Oysters with Garlic Butter (above)

GRILLED OYSTERS WITH GARLIC BUTTER

Illustrated opposite

The romantic and luxurious image of oysters was not always so – they were once the food of the poor. Now, with exciting developments in their production and distribution, they are within the scope of the average household purse again. I love their sea-salty fresh taste totally unadulterated – all you need is a dash of fresh lemon juice or a tasty drop of Tabasco sauce and a few slices of brown bread and butter. But this way of serving them hot is simple and highly recommended – especially with a glass of champagne or alternatively Guinness at hand!

16 oysters
16 thick slices bread (optional)
100 g / 4 oz butter, softened
2 cloves garlic, crushed
3–4 tablespoons roughly chopped parsley
fresh wholemeal breadcrumbs
3 tablespoons freshly grated Parmesan cheese
(optional)
lemon wedges and brown bread and butter to serve

OPEN the oysters (see page 53), arrange the shells with the oysters in a baking dish – taking care not to spill the juice. To keep the oysters upright you could stand them in thick slices of bread in which you have cut out round shapes to cradle the shells and keep them steady. Cream the butter and garlic together, add the parsley and beat in. Put a knob of this butter on each oyster, then a good sprinkling of breadcrumbs. Dot a few tiny pieces of the garlic butter over the breadcrumbs and, if you like, a sprinkling of Parmesan cheese. Grill for no more than 2 minutes. Serve immediately and mop up the lovely juices with brown bread and butter, also offer wedges of lemon for a squeeze of juice to taste. SERVES 4

SMOKED SALMON SOUFFLÉ

a little butter
300 ml/½ pint white sauce (page 172)
3 eggs, separated
100 g/4 oz smoked salmon scraps, chopped
salt and freshly ground black pepper

LIGHTLY butter a soufflé dish. Make the sauce according to the instructions on page 172 and let it cool slightly. Beat in the egg yolks one at a time then add the chopped smoked salmon. Season to taste with salt and pepper.

Whisk the egg whites until stiff and, using a metal spoon, carefully fold into the soufflé mixture. Tip gently into the soufflé dish and bake in a moderate oven (180c, 350f, gas 4) for about 30 minutes, or until the soufflé has risen and set. Serve immediately. SERVES 4

MOULES À LA MARINIÈRE

—————— *Illustrated on page 57* ——————

3.5 litres/6 pints mussels
25 g/1 oz butter
1 onion, finely chopped
300 ml/½ pint dry white wine
1 bay leaf
3 sprigs thyme
3 tablespoons chopped parsley
salt and freshly ground black pepper
1–2 tablespoons chopped parsley to garnish

PREPARE the mussels as described on page 56. Melt the butter over a gentle heat and add the onion. Cook for a few minutes until softened then add the wine, bay leaf, thyme and parsley. Season with black pepper.

Place the mussels in this liquid and cook for about 5 to 10 minutes, or until the shells are open. It is important to remember to discard any mussels which have not opened as these will be inedible. Remove the open mussels with a slotted spoon and keep warm. Strain the liquid and season to taste. Pour over the mussels and sprinkle with chopped parsley to garnish. SERVES 4–6

DEEP-FRIED MONKFISH IN APPLE BATTER

—————— *Illustrated on pages 186–7* ——————

This recipe is taken from *The Apple Book* by Jane Simpson and Gill MacLennan.

450 g/1 lb monkfish
2 tablespoons lemon juice
2 tablespoons flour
salt and freshly ground pepper
oil for deep frying
apple sauce to serve

BATTER
100 g/4 oz plain flour
2 teaspoons baking powder
½ teaspoon salt
freshly ground black pepper
150 ml/¼ pint apple purée
4 tablespoons cider
1 egg

FIRST make the batter. Sift the flour, baking powder, salt and pepper into a bowl. Add the apple purée, cider and egg and beat well together for 1 to 2 minutes, then set aside.

Remove the skin and main bone from the monkfish (see page 48) or ask the fishmonger to do this for you, cut into chunks and place in a bowl with the lemon juice. Mix well, then coat in the flour, salt and pepper.

Heat the oil. Dip the monkfish in the batter and drop 5 pieces at a time into the hot oil. Cook for 5 minutes, until dark golden. Drain on absorbent kitchen paper and keep warm. Repeat with the remaining monkfish and serve immediately with a tart apple sauce. SERVES 4

PRAWN COCKTAIL

Illustrated on page 183

*1 crisp lettuce (Webbs, Iceberg or cos) or
endive
350 g/12 oz peeled cooked prawns
whole prawns and lemon twists to garnish
lemon wedges and brown bread and butter to
serve*

DRESSING
*225 g/8 oz very ripe tomatoes (or small tin of
tomatoes)
2 teaspoons concentrated tomato purée
3 tablespoons mayonnaise (page 181)
3 tablespoons soured cream, quark or natural
yogurt
dash of Tabasco or chilli sauce
freshly ground black pepper*

WASH and pat dry the lettuce, and put it in a polythene bag and chill for an hour or two.

Meanwhile, make the sauce. Peel the tomatoes by putting in a small bowl and pouring over boiling water. Leave for a minutes, then make a small incision in each tomato and the skin should start to come away. Cut the tomatoes in half and deseed. Put into a blender or food processor with the tomato purée, mayonnaise, soured cream, quark or yogurt, and process until well blended. Adjust the amount of tomato purée according to the flavour of the tomatoes, and their colour. Season with a squeeze of lemon juice, a dash of Tabasco or chilli sauce to taste and freshly ground black pepper. The sauce should be a delicate pink colour.

Shred the chilled lettuce, and combine with the prawns and heap into frosted cocktail glasses. Spoon a tablespoon or two of the sauce over each serving and garnish with whole prawns and a twist of fresh lemon. Serve with extra wedges of lemon and thin slices of brown bread with a little butter.
SERVES 4–6

CRAB AND AVOCADO MOUSSE

This delicately flavoured and coloured mousse needs to be served as soon as it has chilled and set as the avocado will lose its colour and flavour if kept for much longer than this. I like to use an ice-cream or potato scoop when serving the mousse – the pale green mousse balls set on individual plates with a garnish of salad are most impressive.

*2 ripe avocados
4 tablespoons soured cream
350 g/12 oz white crab meat, flaked
pinch each of salt and white pepper
squeeze of lemon juice
15 g/½ oz powdered gelatine
6 tablespoons hot water
2 eggs, lightly whisked*

TO SERVE
*1 lettuce, cut into fine ribbons
½ cucumber, diced
3–4 tablespoons Cocktail Sauce (page 182)*

CUT the avocados in half lengthways and remove the stones. Scoop out the flesh, roughly chop and place in a food processor or liquidiser with the soured cream and crab meat then blend until smooth. Season to taste with salt, pepper and a squeeze of lemon juice, then transfer to large glass or china bowl. Dissolve the gelatine in the hot water and allow to cool before stirring into the crab and avocado mixture. Put in the refrigerator until nearly set (about 30 to 60 minutes), then fold in the whisked egg whites. Return the mousse to the refrigerator for about 2 hours, or until set. On individual plates, place two or three scoops of the mousse on a bed of the combined lettuce and cucumber and pour just a little cocktail sauce over the mousse.
SERVES 4–6

Soups and Chowders

There is so much that you can do to make a good fish stock into a delicious, tasty soup. Indeed, some fish soups are so elaborate and full of ingredients that they could be classified almost as stews or casseroles – such as the classic Bouillabaisse (see page 81) – whereas other soups can be clear, fragrant and delicate in flavour, providing a wonderful introduction to a meal.

Experiment with vegetables and fresh herbs in season to create your own soups, chowders or bisques. There is enormous scope for your own personal touch. Full-blooded winter soups can be fortified with wine, as in Hearty Fish Soup (see page 81) or try a dash of rum. In the summer you can utilise your food processor or liquidiser to combine natural yogurt, wine, herbs and flaked fish to provide stunning chilled soups. Often you will find that a main meal has provided the basis for a good soup: braises, for example, can be blended; fish heads, tails and scraps can be used for making stock.

This selection of classic soups and chowders sets out the basics for making good soup. Remember that in most cases the fish should be added in the final cooking stages, so you could make the base of your soup well in advance then simply reheat it gently and add the fish just before you are ready to eat. Seasoning should always be checked and adjusted in the final stages.

Prawn and Sweetcorn Chowder (page 85) and Bouillabaisse (page 80)

BOUILLABAISSE

Illustrated on page 78

This is a great French Mediterranean classic. Like the Spanish paella, there are many, many versions and variations – so that it offers great scope to the keen and imaginative cook. It is filling and rich and can be offered as a hearty main course. Use fish according to season and availability – and choose inexpensive shell-fish such as mussels or whatever your fishmonger recommends as a good buy. Whatever combination of ingredients you use, bouillabaisse should always include saffron, garlic, olive oil and tomatoes.

900 g/2 lb mixed fish and shellfish (e.g. firm-fleshed cod, haddock, whiting, coley, ling, John Dory, mussels, peeled cooked prawns or shrimps)
3 tablespoons olive oil
2 onions, chopped
2–3 cloves garlic, crushed
2 sticks celery
3 potatoes, thinly sliced
450 g/1 lb tomatoes, peeled and chopped (see below)
bouquet garni of 2 bay leaves, thyme and parsley
2 pieces orange peel
salt and freshly ground black pepper
pinch of saffron strands or 1 teaspoon saffron powder
Aïoli (page 183), double cream, soured cream or yogurt to serve
1–2 tablespoons chopped parsley to garnish

CLEAN, scale and cut the fish into fairly thick pieces (see page 44). Heat the olive oil in a large, heavy pan and soften the onions and garlic. Add the celery and potatoes and continue cooking for 1 to 2 minutes. Slide in the chopped tomatoes, herbs, orange peel and season, add water with infused saffron and heat up – then add all firmer-fleshed fish, simmer for about 5 minutes. Prepare mussels (see page 56) and add them with their juices – also soft-fleshed fish and prawns. Just cook gently and briefly until all is cooked and still firm. Transfer into a soup tureen, stir in aioli, garnish with the parsley and serve with hot garlic bread or croûtons. SERVES 8–10

To Peel Tomatoes
Place the tomatoes in a heatproof bowl and cover with boiling water. Leave for a few minutes then make a slit in the tomato skins with the point of a sharp knife. The skins should peel off easily.

GENOESE FISH SOUP

25 g/1 oz butter
1 onion, chopped
1 clove garlic, crushed
3 sticks celery, sliced
50 g/2 oz rindless streaky bacon, chopped
1 (397-g/14-oz) can chopped tomatoes
150 ml/¼ pint dry white wine
300 ml/½ pint fish stock (page 170)
½ teaspoon marjoram
salt and black pepper
450 g/1 lb monkfish, cod or coley, boned, skinned and diced (pages 45–8)
100 g/4 oz peeled cooked prawns
2 tablespoons chopped parsley to garnish

MELT the butter in a large saucepan and soften the onion and garlic for 2 to 3 minutes. Add the celery and bacon and continue cooking over a low heat for a few more minutes. Add the tomatoes, wine, stock and seasonings. Simmer for 10 minutes.

Add the fish and cook for 5 minutes. Finally add the prawns and simmer for a further 2 to 3 minutes. Check the seasoning and serve hot, garnished with chopped parsley. SERVES 4–6

LA BOURRIDE

A classic Provençal fish soup with garlic – certainly hearty enough for a main meal. The preparation is rather time consuming, but is well worth the effort. You can use your own choice and combination of fish – I recommend monkfish, perhaps some fillet of turbot – or haddock, cod and halibut. There are many versions of this soup; this is mine.

stock, made with 225 g/8 oz fish trimmings, 2
onions, 2–3 sticks of celery, strips of orange
and lemon peel, 150 ml/¼ pint dry cider or
white wine, and about 600 ml/1 pint water,
salt and freshly ground black pepper
1.5 kg/3 lb firm white fish, filleted
2 leeks, finely sliced
1 onion, finely sliced
3 cloves garlic, 2 crushed
450 g/1 lb potatoes, sliced
½ quantity Aïoli (page 183)
olive oil for frying
1 stick French bread

FIRST, make the stock as described on page 170. Prepare your choice of fish, and arrange in a large pan on top of the leeks, onion, crushed garlic and potatoes. Cover with the stock, and poach for about 10 minutes or until the fish is tender. Keep an eye on the fish as different kinds and thicknesses cook at different speeds – be careful not to let it overcook and break up.

With a perforated spoon or fish slice, transfer the cooked fish and potatoes to a heated dish and keep warm. Reduce the remaining stock in the pan down to one third of the quantity, let it cool slightly, then strain slowly and carefully into the aioli, beating all the time. Then gently heat this soup in a saucepan, but do not allow it to boil. Rub a frying pan with the remaining clove of garlic, and heat up the olive oil. Fry thick slices of French bread and place a slice or two in the bottom of individual soup bowls. Place the reserved fish and potatoes on top and ladle over the soup. Serve immediately. SERVES 8

HEARTY FISH SOUP

Illustrated on page 171

This soup can be prepared in advance to the stage where you add the fish.

2 tablespoons olive oil
3–4 cloves garlic, crushed
2 large onions, chopped
2 leeks, sliced
2 large carrots, thinly sliced
1 (425-g/15-oz) can chopped tomatoes
900 ml/1½ pints fish stock (page 170)
300 ml/½ pint white wine
bouquet garni of bay leaf, parsley and thyme
juice and rind of 1 orange
salt and freshly ground black pepper
900 g/2 lb assorted mixed fish or fish fillets,
according to season
4 tablespoons double cream or thick-set
natural yogurt
whole prawns and 1 tablespoon chopped
parsley to garnish

HEAT the olive oil in a large, deep, heavy saucepan and soften down the crushed garlic and onion. Add the leeks, and carrots and cook for another 1 to 2 minutes. Tip in the tomatoes, stock, wine, herbs, orange juice and rind. Season to taste and simmer for about 15 minutes.

Meanwhile, clean and prepare the fish, and cut into bite-sized pieces. Add the firm white fish and cook for 3 to 4 minutes, then add the softer-fleshed fish and cook for a further 2 or 3 minutes – adding any prawns for the last minute or so.

Pour the soup into a tureen, swirl in the cream or yogurt and float a few whole, unpeeled prawns on top. Garnish with chopped parsley. SERVES 6

LOBSTER BISQUE

Having splashed out on lobster or crawfish –
and thoroughly enjoyed it – you will be
delighted to know that there is yet more to
come! The pounded shells of these shellfish
can produce a lovely stock, from which I have
devised this extremely elegant soup.

25 g/1 oz butter or oil
2 medium carrots, roughly chopped
1 stick celery, chopped
1 onion, roughly chopped
1 lobster or crawfish shell, legs and any scraps
of left-over flesh
6 black peppercorns
salt
1 small bunch parsley
2–3 teaspoons coarsely chopped mint
1 tablespoon double cream

IN a large, heavy saucepan, melt the butter or
heat the oil and sweat out the prepared
vegetables for 5 to 7 minutes. Break up the
shells and legs of the lobster or crawfish and
pack on top of the vegetables. Just cover with
water and add the peppercorns, salt and
parsley. Gently simmer for 30 to 45 minutes.

Strain this stock into a bowl. Add 2 to 3
teaspoons of freshly chopped mint leaves and
stir in the double cream. Add also any
reserved flakes of shellfish if you have them.
Chill and serve with mint leaves floating on
top as garnish. Or, very gently reheat and
serve with fresh warmed bread. SERVES 4

MUSSEL AND TOMATO SOUP

You can add a couple of tablespoons of freshly grated Parmesan to this simple, earthy soup, if you wish.

3 cloves garlic, crushed
1 large onion, chopped
4 tablespoons olive oil
1 (397-g/14-oz) can chopped tomatoes
300 ml/½ pint dry white wine
1 teaspoon oregano
salt and freshly ground black pepper
2.25 litres/4 pints mussels
2 tablespoons double cream
2 tablespoons chopped parsley to garnish

SOFTEN the garlic and onion in the olive oil then add the tomatoes, dry white wine, oregano and seasoning to taste. Simmer for about 10 minutes.

Meanwhile, scrub and prepare the mussels (see page 56), put them into the soup and let them gently steam open. Remember to discard any mussels which do not open. After a few minutes, stir in the double cream and add a little more wine if the soup is too thick.

Serve in large soup bowls with a garnish of chopped parsley. Use your fingers to scoop up the soup with the halved shells of the mussels and mop up the juices with very fresh bread. SERVES 4–6

Fish Soup with Dumplings

This is a clear fish soup which is light and refreshing. Adding the trimmings from smoked fish improves the flavour and colour of the soup.

600 ml/1 pint fish stock (page 170)
175 g/6 oz bones and flakes of smoked haddock or other smoked fish

Dumplings
50 g/2 oz fresh breadcrumbs
1 tablespoon chopped parsley
50 g/2 oz cooked white fish or smoked haddock fillets, skinned and flaked
½ teaspoon grated lemon rind
50 g/2 oz butter, softened
1 egg yolk
freshly ground white pepper

ADD the smoked haddock when making the fish stock as described on page 170.

To make the dumplings, combine all the ingredients and form into very small dumplings (makes about 20) and chill them in the refrigerator for 1 hour. Strain the stock, then bring it to the boil and turn it down to simmer. Drop the dumplings in and poach for 15 to 20 minutes. Serve immediately. SERVES 4

Surimi Soup

Illustrated on page 171

350 g/12 oz white fish fillets, skinned (page 49)
fresh ground black pepper
1 tablespoon freshly chopped parsley
1.15 litres/2 pints fish stock (page 170)
225 g/8 oz cucumber, partially skinned and sliced
100 g/4 oz button mushrooms, thinly sliced
1 tablespoon soy sauce
2 tablespoons freshly chopped celery leaves
prawn crackers to serve (optional)

BLEND, liquidise or finely chop the fish and season with the pepper and parsley. Refrigerate until firm. Shape the fish mixture into small 2.5-cm/1-in balls. Refrigerate until required. Meanwhile, bring the stock to the boil, carefully add the fish balls and simmer for 5 minutes. Add the cucumber and mushrooms and continue cooking for a further 5 to 8 minutes, until the fish balls are tender. Add the soy sauce. Serve sprinkled with celery leaves and accompanied with prawn crackers, if wished. SERVES 6

Chilled Avocado and Smoked Haddock Soup

450 g/1 lb smoked haddock fillet
milk, lemon and herb stock (page 170)
2 ripe avocados
about 300 ml/½ pint fish stock (page 170)
salt and freshly ground white pepper
1 tablespoon natural yogurt (optional)
mint leaves to garnish

POACH the smoked haddock fillets in the milk stock for about 5 minutes, using just enough barely to cover the fillets. Remove from the heat and allow to cool. Reserve the poaching liquid and strain. Skin the haddock fillets and roughly flake. Put into a food processor or liquidiser. Peel the avocado, remove the stone and chop, then add to the bowl with the strained poaching liquid. Blend until smooth then transfer to a large glass or china bowl. With a balloon whisk, stir in sufficient fish stock to thin down the mixture to a creamy soup consistency. Check the seasoning and, if you like, add a tablespoon of yogurt at this stage. Chill the soup before serving. Do not keep as the avocados will lose their colour and flavour if not served fairly soon. Garnish the individual bowls of chilled soup with whole mint leaves and serve with chilled white wine and good fresh bread. SERVES 3–4

PRAWN AND SWEETCORN CHOWDER

Illustrated on page 78

1 large onion, chopped
1 green pepper, deseeded and chopped
2 tablespoons oil
450 g / 1 lb potatoes, peeled and diced
900 ml / 1½ pints fish stock (page 170)
350 g / 12 oz white fish, skinned and cut into bite-sized pieces
225 g / 8 oz peeled cooked prawns
225 g / 8 oz sweetcorn
salt and freshly ground pepper
1–2 tablespoons chopped parsley and whole prawns to garnish

SOFTEN the chopped onion and green pepper in the oil for a few minutes, then add the potatoes. Pour in the stock and simmer gently for 10 minutes. Add the fish and cook for 5 minutes, then add the prawns and sweetcorn and continue cooking for 3 to 4 minutes. Season to taste with salt and pepper and garnish with the chopped parsley and a few whole unpeeled prawns. SERVES 4–6

FISHERMAN'S CHOWDER

50 g / 2 oz butter
1 large onion, thinly sliced
100 g / 4 oz rindless bacon, chopped
4 sticks celery, chopped
1 small red or green pepper, deseeded and diced
1 large potato, peeled and diced
300 ml / ½ pint fish stock (page 170)
675 g / 1½ lb smoked and white fish (e.g. cod, coley, smoked haddock), skinned and cubed
300 ml / ½ pint milk
1 tablespoon cornflour
salt and freshly ground black pepper

MELT the butter in a large saucepan. Cook the onion, bacon, celery, pepper and potato for 5 minutes.

Add the stock and simmer until the potatoes are just tender then add the fish to the pan.

Blend the milk and cornflour, stir into the pan, bring to the boil, stirring occasionally, and simmer for 5 minutes.

Season before serving with salt and pepper to taste. SERVES 6

COD AND KIPPER CHOWDER

This is a truly delicious soup, and I like to add some prawns in the finishing stages to enhance the lovely fresh sea fish taste.

25 g / 1 oz butter
1 medium onion, finely chopped
600 ml / 1 pint fish stock (page 170)
600 ml / 1 pint milk
2–3 potatoes, scrubbed and diced
275 g / 10 oz cod fillet, skinned and cut into small, bite-sized pieces (page 49)
275 g / 10 oz kipper fillet, skinned and cut into small, bite-sized pieces
100 g / 4 oz peeled cooked prawns (optional)
squeeze of lemon juice
freshly ground pepper

MELT the butter in a large heavy pan over a gentle heat and slowly sweat out the finely chopped onion until pale and soft. Add the stock and milk and bring up to just gently simmering, then add the diced potato. Simmer (do not boil) for about 5 to 8 minutes, until the potato is half cooked through, then add the pieces of cod and continue to cook for a further 2 to 3 minutes. Add the kipper, prawns, if using, and continue to cook gently until they are heated through. Check the seasoning. The kipper and your fish stock should obviate the need for further salt, but you can add a squeeze of lemon juice and a sprinkle of pepper to taste. Serve with warm bread rolls. SERVES 6

Main Courses

Considering that we are a nation of islanders surrounded by a wealth of wonderful seafood, it is surprising to me how few cooks consider using fish as a main course – especially when entertaining.

Just imagine a beautiful baked sea bass, so simple to cook, stunning to behold and superb in taste and texture. Think of the silvery skin of herring, the greeney-blue back of the handsome mackerel, quickly grilled and served with an elegant dish of salad and pretty fruit sauce – what could be more appealing to the eye, easy on the purse and delicious to eat? And take a glorious fish like Dover sole, (no relation to lemon sole, incidentally), or John Dory or halibut or turbot – all examples of fish so superior in taste that it is rarely necessary to do more than simply grill, bake or steam them for perfect results.

I prefer my fresh fish dishes cooked in the simplest manner and I like to keep accompanying sauces and vegetables as simple and as fresh as possible. However, I have included many favourite classics in this chapter, as well as some new ideas – but do remember to be adventurous and substitute species of fish according to season and availability. Above all, remember that the secret of successful fish cookery is never ever to overcook your fish.

Brill and Mushrooms with Lemon Sauce (page 88)
and Red Mullet with Orange and Fennel (page 104)

STUFFED SEA BREAM WITH FENNEL SAUCE

Illustrated on pages 174–5

1 sea bream
1 tablespoon oil

STUFFING
25 g/1 oz butter
1 clove garlic, finely chopped
2 carrots, cut into matchsticks
1 stick celery, cut into matchsticks
4 leeks, white part only, sliced lengthways
1 tablespoons chopped parsley

SAUCE
1 shallot
50 g/2 oz butter
50 g/2 oz wholemeal flour
1 bulb fennel, grated
300 ml/$\frac{1}{2}$ pint fish stock (page 170) or white wine
salt and freshly ground pepper
2–3 tablespoons double cream or fromage blanc

ASK the fishmonger to clean the fish, scale and trim off the fins (or see page 44). To make the stuffing, melt the butter in a saucepan and gently cook the garlic and prepared vegetables. Put these into the belly of the bream and place the fish on a lightly greased roasting tin. Brush with a little oil and bake in a hot oven (220 C, 425 F, gas 7) for about 15 minutes.

Meanwhile, make the sauce by finely chopping the shallot, and softening it in the butter over a gentle heat. Add the flour and cook gently for a further 1 to 2 minutes. Add the grated fennel, fish stock or white wine gradually and cook until the sauce is thickened, then season to taste. Remove from the heat and swirl in the double cream or fromage blanc. Present the bream on a heated serving dish, allowing the vegetable stuffing to fall out and form a garnish. Serve the sauce separately. SERVES 4

BRILL AND MUSHROOMS WITH LEMON SAUCE

Illustrated on page 86

4 brill fillets
100 g/4 oz mushrooms
50 g/2 oz butter
salt and freshly ground black pepper
juice of $\frac{1}{2}$ lemon
4 tablespoons white wine

SAUCE
juice of $\frac{1}{2}$ lemon
2 tablespoons chopped parsley
300 ml/$\frac{1}{2}$ pint fish stock (page 170)
1 tablespoon flour
2 eggs

WASH and pat dry the fillets; skin (see page 49) or leave as they are, as you prefer. Cut the mushrooms into thin slices. Lightly butter an ovenproof dish and arrange the mushrooms on the base. Fold the fillets in half and lay them on top of the mushrooms. Season, and squeeze lemon juice over them. Add enough wine to moisten the mushrooms and dot the top of the fillets with a few knobs of the butter. Bake in a moderate oven (180 c, 350 F, gas 4) for 20 minutes, until the fillets are tender.

Put all the sauce ingredients into the bowl of a food processor or blender and process until smooth. Pour into the top of a double boiler, or into a bowl that sits over a saucepan of simmering water: do not let the bowl touch the water. Whisk the sauce constantly over a low heat until it thickens, then season and add a little of the cooking juices from the brill dish. Arrange folded fillets of brill carefully on a warmed serving dish, pour over some of the sauce and sprinkle the mushrooms over the top. Serve the remaining sauce separately. SERVES 4

COD STEAKS À LA GRECQUE

1 onion, finely chopped
1 clove garlic, crushed
a little olive oil
1 (57-g/2-oz) can concentrated tomato purée
150 ml/¼ pint fish stock (page 170)
6 green and 6 black olives, stoned
2 tablespoons dry sherry
salt and freshly ground black pepper
4 cod steaks
a few olives and watercress sprigs to garnish

GENTLY cook the onion and garlic in a little olive oil until transparent, but do not brown. Add the tomato purée, fish stock, olives, sherry and season to taste. Arrange the cod steaks in a lightly greased ovenproof dish, and pour the sauce over and around them. Bake in a moderate oven (180 c, 350 f, gas 4) for 20 to 25 minutes, then garnish with olives and watercress and serve immediately. SERVES 4

COD IN COCONUT AND APPLE SAUCE

I love the idea of fish with fruit and this recipe from *The Apple Book* by Jane Simpson and Gill McLennan is particularly tasty.

2 tablespoons oil
1 large onion, finely chopped
2 medium cooking apples
75 g/3 oz creamed or shredded coconut
1 teaspoon salt
1 teaspoon sugar
300 ml/½ pint fish stock (page 170)
2 teaspoons Madras curry powder
2 teaspoons ground coriander
1 teaspoon ground cumin
675 g/1½ lb cod fillets, skinned (page 49)

PLACE the oil in a large pan, add the onion and cook over a medium heat for 5 to 7 minutes, until the onion is softened and lightly browned. Peel, core and slice the apples into the pan. Add the coconut to the pan with the salt, sugar, stock, curry powder, coriander and cumin. Bring to the boil, cover and simmer for 20 minutes, stirring occasionally to prevent sticking. Process until smooth in a food processor or liquidiser and return to the pan. Cut the cod into large chunks. Add to the sauce and simmer, uncovered, for 10 minutes until the cod flakes easily when pressed with a knife. Serve with plain boiled rice mixed with peas. SERVES 4–6

CHILLED MARINATED COD STEAKS

4 cod steaks
a little oil
parsley or tarragon sprigs to garnish

MARINADE
150 ml/¼ pint dry white wine
6 tablespoons white wine vinegar
2 cloves garlic, crushed
12 cloves
juice and rind of 2 oranges and 2 lemons
bouquet garni of parsley, tarragon, thyme and bay leaf
salt and freshly ground black pepper

GENTLY fry the cod steaks in a little oil for a few minutes on each side. Lift them out of the pan carefully, with a fish slice or spatula, and arrange on the base of a dish suitable to hold the marinade. Make up the marinade with the listed ingredients and pour into the fish juices in the pan. Stir as you bring the marinade up to the boil then simmer for 5 minutes to extract the aroma and flavour of the herbs and spices. Pour over the cod steaks to cover completely. Cool, cover with cling film then refrigerate overnight.

To serve, lift the cod steaks on to a serving dish, and pour over the strained marinade. Garnish with parsley sprigs or fresh tarragon. SERVES 4

SEA BASS WITH GINGER AND SPRING ONION

A beautiful, silvery fish – rather similar in shape to salmon but more bony. The flesh is quite tender, so this fish responds well to baking. This recipe is typically Chinese in its use of ingredients – especially the combination of root ginger with spring onions.

1 medium sea bass, cleaned
pinch each of salt and sugar
1 tablespoon sesame oil
1 tablespoon soy sauce
1 bunch spring onions
2 large cloves garlic
2 ($3\frac{1}{2}$cm/$1\frac{1}{2}$in) pieces of fresh root ginger

GARNISH
6 spring onions
lime slices

RUB the sea bass with the salt, sugar, sesame oil and soy sauce. Chop the spring onions, garlic and ginger, and put half of these ingredients in a layer on the bottom of a lightly greased sheet of aluminium foil. Place the sea bass on top, and cover with the remaining mixture. Parcel up loosely, and bake in a moderate oven (180 c, 350 f, gas 4) for 20 minutes or until tender. Serve with a garnish of frilled spring onions and slices of lime in its own cooking juices. SERVES 3–4

COD CATALAN

For a change you could use conger eel steaks in place of the cod used in this recipe.

25 g / 1 oz butter
1 large onion, sliced
1 clove garlic, crushed
25 g / 1 oz flour
1 (397-g / 14-oz) can chopped tomatoes
1 tablespoon concentrated tomato purée
50 g / 2 oz stuffed olives, halved
2 (225-g / 8-oz) cod steaks
juice of $\frac{1}{2}$ lemon
salt and freshly ground black pepper

GARNISH
25 g / 1 oz hazelnuts, chopped
1 tablespoon freshly chopped parsley

MELT the butter in a pan and lightly sauté the onion and garlic until soft. Sprinkle on the flour and stir in the tomatoes and tomato purée. Bring to the boil, stirring continuously. Pour into an ovenproof dish and stir in the olives.

Sprinkle the cod steaks with lemon juice and season with salt and pepper. Place in the tomato mixture. Cover and bake in a moderately hot oven (190 C, 375 F, gas 5) for 25 minutes. Just before serving, sprinkle with hazelnuts and parsley. SERVES 2

COLEY AUBERGINES

Illustrated on pages 30–1

Any firm white fish may be used for this dish.

*2 medium aubergines
salt and freshly ground black pepper
450 g / 1 lb coley fillets
50 g / 2 oz butter
juice of 1 lemon
2 courgettes, diced
1 onion, chopped
2 cloves garlic, crushed
1 tablespoon oil
225 g / 8 oz tomatoes, peeled and chopped
(page 80)
1 teaspoon oregano or basil
100 g / 4 oz Cheddar or Gruyère cheese, grated*

CUT the aubergines in half lengthways, score the flesh, sprinkle with salt and leave to sweat for 30 minutes. Meanwhile, season the fish fillets, dot with a little butter, squeeze over a little lemon juice and parcel in foil. Bake in a moderate oven (180 c, 350 f, gas 4) for 15 to 20 minutes until cooked.

Wash the salt off the aubergines and pat dry. Place, flesh side down, on a lightly greased baking dish and bake in a moderately hot oven (200 c, 400 f, gas 6) for about 40 minutes, until the flesh is tender. Allow to cool slightly, then run a sharp knife around the edge of the flesh and skin and scoop the flesh out. Put the aubergine flesh into a mixing bowl and chop, then mash with a fork. Soften the courgette, onion and garlic in the remaining 25 g / 1 oz butter and the oil. Add the chopped tomatoes to the aubergine, and stir in the courgette mixture, the herbs and the flaked coley, season with salt and pepper and pile the mixture back in the aubergine shells. Top with the grated cheese and bake in a hot oven (220 c, 425 f, gas 7) for 10 to 15 minutes, until brown and bubbling. SERVES 4

MEDITERRANEAN-STYLE COLEY

Illustrated on page 19

You could also use ling or huss for this quick and simple dish.

*1 onion, chopped
1 clove garlic, crushed
25 g / 1 oz butter, melted
2 tomatoes, roughly chopped
225 g / 8 oz courgettes, sliced
1 tablespoon concentrated tomato purée
1 teaspoon marjoram
pinch each of salt and freshly ground black
pepper
675 g / 1½ lb coley fillets, skinned (page 49) and
cut into bite-sized pieces*

COOK the onion and garlic gently in butter for a few minutes until pale and soft. Mix in all the ingredients except the coley and cook gently for 10 to 15 minutes, until the courgettes are tender. Then add the coley, and continue cooking for a further 10 minutes. Serve immediately, perhaps accompanied by brown rice. SERVES 4

CONGER PIE

Down here on the Isles of Scilly, there was an old rhyme which went . . . 'Scads and tatties all the week, and Conger Pie on Sunday' (scads are fish!). The islanders prized conger eel more then than now, which is a pity because the flesh is firm and has a good strong flavour. You could substitute other firm white fish for this pie.

675–900 g/1½–2 lb conger eel
300 ml/½ pint fish stock (page 170)
250 ml/8 fl oz red wine
2 large onions, chopped
2 cloves garlic, crushed
2 tablespoons oil
40 g/1½ oz flour (optional)
50 g/2 oz butter (optional)

TOPPING
675 g/1½ lb potatoes, peeled and boiled
2 tablespoons milk
3 eggs, separated
salt and freshly ground black pepper
2 tablespoons chopped parsley
50 g/2 oz Cheddar cheese, grated
cayenne

CUT the conger eel into steaks, or ask your fishmonger to do this for you. Poach them in the stock and wine (see pages 24–5) until tender. Remove the steaks with a slotted spoon and, while the stock continues to simmer and reduce, peel off the skin of the eel and remove the bones to leave chunks of flesh. Soften the onions and garlic in a little oil then transfer to a deep pie or soufflé dish. Arrange the eel on top of this. The stock can be further thickened, if you like, with beurre manie (the flour kneaded into the butter). Drop in small knobs of beurre manie one at a time, stirring until the sauce thickens. Check the seasoning and pour the sauce over the fish and onions.

To make the topping, mash the potatoes very thoroughly until they are absolutely smooth. Add the milk and egg yolks, season with a pinch each of salt and freshly ground black pepper and add the chopped parsley.

Beat thoroughly. Whisk the egg whites until stiff and fold into the potatoes.

Spoon the potato mixture over the pie, sprinkle with the grated cheese and a dusting of cayenne and bake in a moderately hot oven (200 c, 400 f, gas 6) for 20 minutes. Serve with green vegetables in season. SERVES 6

EEL-PIE ISLAND PIE

675 g/1½ lb eel
75 g/3 oz butter
1 onion, finely chopped
3 tablespoons chopped parsley
pinch of freshly grated nutmeg
3 tablespoons dry sherry
salt and freshly ground black pepper
2–3 hard-boiled eggs, roughly chopped
50 g/2 oz flour
juice of 1 lemon
225 g/8 oz puff pastry, defrosted if frozen
1 egg, beaten, to glaze

SKIN and bone the eel and cut into large pieces, or ask your fishmonger to do this for you. Melt 25 g/1 oz butter in a large saucepan and gently soften the finely chopped onion. Add the parsley, nutmeg and sherry, then add the eel and sufficient water just to cover. Season lightly with salt and pepper. Bring slowly to the boil then, once at boiling point, remove the eel with a slotted spoon and place in a greased 1.25 litres/2 pints pie dish. Mix in the roughly chopped egg.

Blend the remaining butter with the flour to form a paste (beurre manie) and drop this into the eel liquid a little at a time. Bring this sauce to the boil, add the lemon juice and check the seasoning. Pour the thickened sauce into the pie dish.

Roll out the pastry to make a lid and cover the pie dish. Brush with beaten egg and decorate, if liked, with any left-over pastry pieces. Bake in a hot oven (220 c, 425 f, gas 7) for 15 minutes, then reduce the temperature to moderately hot (190 f, 375 f, gas 5) for a further 30 minutes. SERVES 6

CRAB-STUFFED HADDOCK

Illustrated opposite

This recipe is taken from *The Long Island Seafood Cookbook* by J. George Frederick.

1 (1.5-kg/3-lb) haddock
2 tablespoons melted butter

STUFFING
350 g/12 oz crab meat, flaked
50 g/2 oz celery, finely chopped
75 g/3 oz cooked apple, finely chopped
1 tablespoon chopped green pepper
1 tablespoon finely chopped pimento
50 g/2 oz fresh breadcrumbs
1 egg, lightly beaten

GARNISH
4 sprigs parsley
1 lime, sliced

CLEAN and wash the haddock then dry thoroughly. Mix together the crab meat and other ingredients for the stuffing and stuff the fish. Place in a baking dish and brush with the melted butter. Bake in a moderate oven (180c, 350f, gas 4) for 55 minutes. Garnish with the parsley and slices of lime. SERVES 6

HADDOCK IN A CURRY AND YOGURT SAUCE

Illustrated opposite

675 g/1½ lb haddock fillets, skinned (page 49)
1 onion, sliced
1 clove garlic, crushed
25 g/1 oz butter
350 g/12 oz long-grain rice, cooked, to serve

MARINADE AND SAUCE
2 tablespoons lemon juice
1 teaspoon honey
pinch each of salt and freshly ground black pepper
2 teaspoons curry powder
300 ml/½ pint natural yogurt
pinch of turmeric
1 teaspoon ground coriander seeds
2 teaspoons grated fresh root ginger
25 g/1 oz butter (optional)

COMBINE the marinade ingredients in a large glass or earthenware bowl. Cut the fish into thick slices and put into the marinade. Cover with cling film and leave in a cool place for 1 to 2 hours.

Gently cook the sliced onion and crushed garlic in the butter, then place in the base of a lightly buttered baking dish. Arrange the fish with its marinade over the onion, cover with a lid or aluminium foil, and bake in a moderate oven (180c, 350f, gas 4) for 30 minutes or until the fish is tender. Have ready a serving dish filled with the plain boiled rice, heaped up around the edge to make a rim, and lift the pieces of fish out of the dish and arrange in the centre of the rice. Transfer the marinade/sauce to a small saucepan and heat gently, adding a few knobs of butter if you wish. Pour the sauce over the fish and serve immediately. SERVES 4–6

Crab-stuffed Haddock (above) and Haddock in a Curry and Yogurt Sauce (above)

HAKE FLORENTINE

75 g/3 oz butter
salt and freshly ground black pepper
4 hake cutlets (or cod, haddock, coley, etc.)
squeeze of lemon juice
675 g/1½ lb spinach
1 onion, finely chopped
1 clove garlic, crushed
25 g/1 oz wholemeal flour
300 ml/½ pint skimmed milk
2 tomatoes, sliced
100 g/4 oz Gruyère cheese, grated
paprika

LIGHTLY butter a sheet of aluminium foil. Season the hake cutlets, sprinkle with a squeeze of lemon juice and top with a few knobs of butter. Place in the foil and parcel up. Place on a baking tray and bake in a moderate oven (180 c, 350 f, gas 4) for 20 minutes or until just tender.

Cook the spinach in boiling water for 3 to 4 minutes then drain and squeeze out all the moisture. Chop finely. Melt 25 g/1 oz of the butter and gently cook the onion and garlic. Cool slightly and mix into the finely chopped spinach.

Make the sauce with the remaining 25 g/1 oz butter, flour and milk and add the juices from the cooked cutlets. Make a base of spinach in an ovenproof dish which has been lightly greased, and make four dents in this base in which to place the cutlets. Cover with the sauce and make an overlapping line of sliced tomatoes over the dish. Top with the grated cheese and a sprinkling of paprika then brown under a grill or bake in a hot oven (220 c, 425 f, gas 7) for 8 to 10 minutes until golden and bubbling. SERVES 4

HAKE WITH HORSERADISH STUFFING

4 hake fillets
3 tablespoons freshly grated horseradish
150 ml/¼ pint natural yogurt
2 tablespoons mayonnaise (page 181)
squeeze of lemon juice
salt and freshly ground black pepper

SKIN the hake fillets (see page 49). Combine all the remaining ingredients and spread a generous amount along each fillet. (Reserve any remaining sauce.) Roll up the fillets towards the tail end, and arrange in a lightly buttered baking dish. Bake in a moderate oven (180 c, 350 f, gas 4) for 20 minutes. Serve on warmed plates with the reserved sauce on the side. SERVES 4

JOHN DORY WITH WINE

1 medium John Dory
50 g/2 oz butter
150 ml/¼ pint dry white wine
2 tablespoons quark or low-fat curd cheese
salt and freshly ground pepper

CUT the fish into 4 fillets (see page 47). Leave the skin on the fillets to help keep them in shape. Heat the butter in a heavy frying pan and cook the fillets gently on both sides for 2 minutes. Turn down the heat, add the wine and cook gently for another 10 minutes. Transfer the fish to a warm serving dish. Reduce the liquid, cool slightly, stir in the quark and season to taste with salt and pepper. Pour over the fillets and serve immediately with tiny new potatoes and with a side salad, if liked. SERVES 2

MARINATED HERRING WITH BLACKBERRY SAUCE

Illustrated on page 178

4 medium herring
1 onion, roughly chopped
10 cloves
2 bay leaves
parsley and thyme
pinch of salt
crushed peppercorns
juice of 2 lemons
300 ml/½ pint white wine vinegar
300 ml/½ pint water
mint sprigs to garnish (optional)

BLACKBERRY SAUCE
2 dessert apples
225 g/8 oz blackberries
1 tablespoon sugar
3 tablespoons red wine
½ teaspoon ground cinnamon
2 cloves
2 tablespoons of the cooking juice/marinade
from the herring
2 tablespoons natural yogurt

CLEAN, wash, bone and split the fish (see pages 44–7). Place in a large baking dish, sprinkle with the onion, seasonings and lemon juice then pour over the wine vinegar and water. Bake in a moderate oven (180 C, 350 F, gas 4) for 20 to 25 minutes. Using a perforated spoon, lift out the fish and arrange on a serving dish. The dish can be served warm or chilled. Garnish with sprigs of mint, if wished, and serve accompanied by the blackberry sauce.

To make the sauce peel, core and chop the apples. Bring the blackberries, apple and sugar to the boil in a little water then add the wine, spices and fish liquid. Cook gently for about 5 minutes. Swirl in the natural yogurt and chill. SERVES 4

HUSS WITH ALMONDS AND APPLE

Illustrated on pages 98–9

Serve this dish with mangetout and plain new, boiled potatoes.

450–675 g/1–1½ lb huss fillets
150 ml/¼ pint milk
pinch each of salt and freshly ground
black pepper
2–3 tablespoons flour
1 tablespoon oil
1 tablespoon butter
100 g/4 oz almonds, sliced
100 g/4 oz dessert apple, peeled, cored and
diced
2 tablespoons double cream
2 tablespoons natural yogurt
pinch of freshly grated nutmeg
1 bunch spring onions, thinly sliced, to garnish

CUT the fish into bite-sized pieces. Dip first in the milk then lightly dust in seasoned flour. Sauté in hot oil and butter in a heavy frying pan (see page 29). Drain on absorbent kitchen paper and transfer to a heated serving plate.

Stir the almonds and diced apple into the pan juices and continue frying until lightly browned, then remove the pan from the heat and stir in the double cream and yogurt, scraping the bottom of the pan to incorporate all the cooking juices. Add the nutmeg and stir until well blended. Pour over the fish and serve immediately with a garnish of finely sliced spring onions. SERVES 4

Mackerel with Lemon and Rosemary (page 100), Smoked Mackerel with Stir-fried Vegetables (page 100) and Huss with Almonds and Apple (above)

MACKEREL WITH TOMATO AND CUCUMBER SAUCE

Illustrated on page 27

6 tomatoes
1 cucumber
1 onion, finely chopped
2–3 tablespoons white wine vinegar
300 ml/½ pint water
2–3 drops of Tabasco sauce
salt and freshly ground pepper
4 medium mackerel, cleaned

PEEL the tomatoes, remove the pips and dice (see page 80). Peel the cucumber, cut in half lengthways, scoop out the pips and dice. Place the diced tomatoes and cucumber in a saucepan with the onion, vinegar, water, Tabasco and seasoning to taste. Simmer for about 25 minutes.

Meanwhile, make 3 or 4 diagonal slashes on each side of the mackerel. (De-head and tail them also if you prefer.) Season them with a pinch of salt and pepper and grill for 4 to 6 minutes on each side, depending on their thickness. Serve immediately. SERVES 4

MACKEREL WITH LEMON AND ROSEMARY

Illustrated on pages 98–9

4 mackerel
4 sprigs fresh or 2 teaspoons dried rosemary
salt and freshly ground black pepper
juice and rind of 2–3 lemons
2 tablespoons butter or oil

CLEAN the mackerel (see page 44), or ask your fishmonger to do this for you. Put the rosemary into the belly cavity of the mackerel. Lightly season and sprinkle with a little lemon juice (inside the cavity).

Heat up the butter or oil in a large, heavy frying pan and brown the mackerel on each side for 3 to 4 minutes. Add the remaining lemon juice and rind, then turn down the heat and continue to cook, just under simmering point, for a further 10 minutes or until the fish is tender. Serve immediately with the pan juices poured over. SERVES 4

SMOKED MACKEREL WITH STIR-FRIED VEGETABLES

Illustrated on pages 98–9

The combination of the cold smoked fish with hot crunchy stir-fried vegetables is unusual and quite delightful.

2 tablespoons sunflower oil
6 medium carrots, thickly sliced
225 g/8 oz broccoli, diced
75 g/3 oz mushrooms, thickly sliced
4 boiled potatoes, diced
2 tomatoes, quartered
½ melon, flesh chopped bite-size
salt and freshly ground black pepper
4 hot-smoked mackerel fillets
lemon wedges to serve (optional)

HEAT the oil in a wok or large, heavy, shallow pan. Add the carrots, then the broccoli spears, stir-fry for 30 seconds, then add the mushrooms, potatoes and tomatoes. Continue stir-frying for 1 minute, add the melon and stir in briskly until just heated through. Season to taste and serve immediately with the smoked mackerel, accompanied by wedges of lemon if wished. SERVES 4

STUFFED GREY MULLET

Grey mullet is one of my favourite fish – but does not seem to be generally very well-known and recipes for this handsome fish are hard to come by. This recipe uses ordinary ingredients in a creative way – the resulting dish looks as though you have spent hours in the kitchen, and yet the preparation is very simple and easy.

1 (1.5-kg/3-lb) grey mullet
75 g/3 oz fresh breadcrumbs
1 tablespoon chopped parsley
2 tablespoons finely chopped onion
3 bay leaves, crumbled
grated rind and juice of 1 lemon
salt and freshly ground black pepper
1 egg, beaten
1 lettuce (preferably Webb's Wonder)
450 g/1 lb potatoes
150 ml/¼ pint dry cider
1 lemon, sliced
a little butter
1 tablespoon crème fraîche or natural yogurt

ASK your fishmonger to scale, clean and bone the mullet, or tackle the operation yourself (see pages 44–5) – it is easier than it looks! – wash and pat dry. Combine the breadcrumbs, chopped parsley, onion, crumbled bay leaves, juice and grated rind of 1 lemon, salt and pepper and bind with beaten egg to make a firm, moist stuffing. Stuff the mullet and set aside.

Blanch the large green outer leaves of the lettuce in boiling salted water for 1 to 2 minutes, drain and pat dry. Parcel up the mullet in these leaves and place in a baking dish. Peel and dice the potatoes and pack around the mullet, season with salt and pepper and pour over the cider. Arrange slices of lemon along the mullet, and dot with little knobs of butter. Bake in a moderate oven (180c, 350f, gas 4) for 35 to 40 minutes. Carefully lift out the mullet and put on a heated serving dish – use a perforated spoon to take the potatoes out and surround the mullet with them. Reduce the cooking juices and swirl in the crème fraîche or yogurt. Peel back the lettuce leaf parcel and pour over the sauce. The fish will slice into beautiful cutlets. Use the heart of the lettuce to make a plain salad. SERVES 2–3

MONKFISH AND VEGETABLE PARCELS WITH SAFFRON SAUCE

450 g/1 lb monkfish
2 medium carrots, cut into matchsticks
2 sticks celery, cut into matchsticks
1 medium onion, very finely sliced into half rings
1 red pepper, deseeded and cut into matchsticks
juice of ½ lemon
3 tablespoons white wine
salt and freshly ground black pepper
4 tablespoons Saffron Sauce (page 177)

CUT four parcels of foil and lightly butter. Skin and bone the monkfish (see page 48) and cut into medallions. In the centre of each parcel, arrange a few medallions of monkfish and surround with small bundles of the prepared vegetables. Sprinkle with lemon juice and the white wine and season lightly. Bring the flap of the parcels over and crimp the edges so that the parcels are totally sealed. Place in a steamer (see page 26) and steam for about 10 minutes or until the fish is tender. The vegetables will be slightly crunchy, and make a lovely contrast to the tender flesh of the monkfish. Meanwhile, prepare the sauce. Turn back the top flap of the parcel to reveal the cooked monkfish and put 1 tablespoon of sauce on each parcel – the juices and sauce will mingle and taste delicious. Serve immediately. SERVES 4

MARINATED MONKFISH KEBABS

The fresh chilled taste of the fruit with the hot kebabs is a wonderful combination.

about 675–900 g / 1½–2 lb monkfish
12–16 bay leaves
12 unshelled cooked prawns
1 endive or crisp lettuce
1 large mango
1 honeydew melon
thinly pared orange and lemon rind to garnish

MARINADE
1 small onion or shallot
juice of 1–2 oranges
juice of 1–2 lemons
equal quantity of olive oil to citrus juice
salt and freshly ground black pepper
2 teaspoons crushed cardamom seeds

PREPARE the monkfish as described on page 48 and cut the flesh into nice chunky cubes. Place in a glass or earthenware bowl. Make the marinade. Chop the onion or shallot finely and add the orange and lemon juice, the same quantity of olive oil, pinch each of salt and pepper, and the crushed cardamom seeds. Give this marinade a stir, and pour over the cubes of monkfish – leave to marinate for 2 hours.

Thread four skewers alternatively with the monkfish, bay leaves, prawns, bay leaves, etc. Turn them slowly as you cook them under a hot grill, or over a barbecue fire, basting all the time with the marinade mixture. Reserve a little of the marinade and use, if liked, as dressing for the salad.

Arrange the kebabs on a platter of endive or crisp shredded lettuce with slices of mango and honeydew melon. Garnish with thinly pared ribbons of orange and lemon rind. SERVES 4–6

PLAICE FILLETS STUFFED WITH COCKLES

The addition of cockles gives this dish a really sea-salty fresh taste!

225 g/8 oz mushrooms
1 medium onion
1 tablespoon fromage blanc
8 plaice fillets, skinned (page 49)
225 g/8 oz fresh cockles (or shellfish as available)
salt and freshly ground black pepper
3 to 4 tablespoons white wine
juice of $\frac{1}{2}$ lemon
50 g/2 oz butter
a good handful wholemeal breadcrumbs
parsley sprigs and lime twists to garnish

FINELY chop the mushrooms and onion, place in a lightly buttered, shallow, fireproof dish and spoon over the fromage blanc. Season the fillets and put a handful of cockles on each one. Roll up from the tail end and arrange these rolled fillets on the vegetable base. Moisten the whole dish with a little white wine and the lemon juice. Melt the butter and pour over the fillets, then scatter with breadcrumbs. Bake in a hot oven (220 c, 425 f, gas 7) for 15 to 20 minutes until golden and bubbling. Garnish the dish with parsley sprigs and twists of thinly sliced lime. SERVES 4

RED MULLET WITH ORANGE AND FENNEL

Illustrated on page 86

This is my favourite way of baking whole mullet either grey or red. Wild fennel (its feathery leaves resemble those of the cultivated bulbs you can buy in the shops) is very common around the seaside and the bruised stalks of this plant give a lovely fragrant taste to all sorts of fish. Try serving it with spinach and parsleyed potatoes.

2 large red mullet
2 bulbs fennel, sliced and poached in a little
water or 2 bunches wild fennel
2 oranges
salt and freshly ground black pepper
50 g / 2 oz butter
halved lime slices (optional), to garnish

CLEAN the whole mullet (see page 44) or ask your fishmonger to do this for you. Arrange a layer of half the poached fennel slices in the bottom of an ovenproof dish and put the mullet on top of this.

Peel the oranges and cut into rounds, reserving any spare juice. Surround and cover the fish with the slices of orange and add any reserved juice, season and cover the fish with the remaining fennel. Dot with butter and bake in a moderately hot oven (200 c, 400 f, gas 6) for about 25 minutes, or until the fish is cooked.

If using wild fennel, bruise and slightly break a few twigs and put the mullet on top, and scatter with the chopped leaves.

Serve immediately, garnished with the oranges and juices from the dish and sprigs of the feathery fennel leaves. You can also use halved slices of lime to garnish to add even more colour to this attractive dish! SERVES 2

GREY MULLET STUFFED WITH PINE NUTS

Illustrated on pages 54–5

Other whole fish, such as pollack, haddock or coley can be substituted for the grey mullet if it is unobtainable.

1 (1.5-kg / 3-lb) grey mullet
3–4 tablespoons natural yogurt or fromage
blanc (optional)

STUFFING
1 onion, finely chopped
100 g / 4 oz pine nuts
2 tablespoons fresh orange juice
100 g / 4 oz chopped apple
$\frac{1}{4}$ teaspoon cinnamon
$\frac{1}{4}$ teaspoon allspice
salt and freshly ground black pepper
2 tablespoons chopped parsley
50 g / 2 oz fresh wholemeal breadcrumbs
1 egg, beaten, to bind
a little dry white wine or cider (optional)

SCALING fish can be done by your fishmonger and ask him to clean the fish too (or see page 44). Prepare the stuffing by mixing all the ingredients listed together and moisten, if necessary, with a little dry white wine or cider. Lightly oil or butter a sheet of aluminium foil, and place the stuffed mullet in the centre. Make a loose parcel around the fish, pouring in a little wine or cider before you seal it. Place on a baking tray or dish and bake in a moderately hot oven (200 c, 400 f, gas 6) for about 25 to 30 minutes, until the flesh is firm and white and comes cleanly away from the bone. Stir the yogurt or fromage blanc into the cooking juices for a delicious sauce, if liked. SERVES 2–3

PLAICE STUFFED WITH SHRIMPS AND SCALLOPS

8 medium scallops
50 g/2 oz butter
150 ml/¼ pint dry white wine
4 medium plaice
150 ml/¼ pint Béchamel Sauce (page 172)
100 g/4 oz peeled cooked prawns
salt and freshly ground black pepper
squeeze of lemon juice
chervil or parsley sprigs to garnish

OPEN the scallops, clean and prepare (see page 53). Slice the white flesh and sauté gently, with the corals, in the butter for 2 minutes, then add the wine and continue to cook for a further 3 or 4 minutes. Remove the scallops with a slotted spoon, separate the corals and reserve with the white flesh, and keep warm on a heated plate.

Bone the plaice for stuffing according to the instructions on page 48 or you can ask your fishmonger to do this. Into the warmed Béchamel Sauce, stir in 3 to 4 tablespoons of stock from the scallops, and mix in the prawns and white flesh of the scallops. Season with salt and pepper to taste. Stuff this mixture into the cavities of the plaice, arrange on a lightly buttered baking dish and squeeze a little lemon juice all over and dot with butter. Bake in a moderate oven (180 c, 350 f, gas 4) for about 20 minutes, until tender. When the fish is cooked, serve on four warmed plates and garnish with the scallop corals, and sprigs of chervil or parsley. SERVES 4

SAVOURY STUFFED PLAICE FILLETS

4 plaice fillets
3 tablespoons dry white wine
25 g/1 oz butter
1–2 tablespoons natural yogurt
grilled tomatoes and watercress sprigs to serve

STUFFING
50 g/2 oz fresh wholemeal breadcrumbs
2 tablespoons finely chopped gherkins
2 tablespoons finely chopped parsley
2 tablespoons finely chopped spring onions,
including green tops
salt and freshly ground black pepper
1 egg, beaten, to bind

COMBINE the stuffing ingredients thoroughly. Place a spoonful of stuffing on each plaice fillet and roll up from head to tail. Arrange on a buttered ovenproof dish, making sure the tail of each fillet is tucked neatly underneath the roll. Add the wine, dot each fillet with a tiny knob of butter and bake in a moderately hot oven (200 c, 400 f, gas 6) for 15 to 20 minutes. Transfer the fillets to a warm serving dish. Reduce the cooking juices in a saucepan, add the yogurt then pour the sauce over the fillets. Surround with grilled tomatoes and sprigs of watercress. SERVES 2

FISH COBBLER

Illustrated opposite

675 g / 1½ lb huss, coley or whiting fillets,
skinned (page 49)
1 onion, chopped
1 clove garlic, crushed
1 tablespoon oil
25 g / 1 oz butter
2 carrots, thinly sliced
2 courgettes, sliced
2 sticks celery, finely sliced
1 (397-g / 14-oz) can tomatoes or
675 g / 1½ lb ripe fresh tomatoes, roughly chopped
1 tablespoon chopped fresh green herbs or
1 teaspoon dried parsley and thyme
1 bay leaf
about 150 ml / ¼ pint fish or vegetable stock
(page 170) or white wine
salt and freshly ground pepper
75 g / 3 oz Cheddar or Parmesan cheese, grated

SCONES
100 g / 4 oz wholemeal flour
100 g / 4 oz plain flour
4 teaspoons baking powder
pinch of salt
50 g / 2 oz butter or margarine
1 tablespoon chopped fresh or 1 teaspoon dried
parsley
1 tablespoon chopped fresh or 1 teaspoon dried
thyme
¼ teaspoon paprika
a little milk to mix

CUT the fish fillets into bite-sized pieces. In a heavy saucepan, soften the onion and garlic in the oil and butter over a gentle heat. Add the carrots, courgettes and celery and continue to cook for about 10 minutes, stirring occasionally. Add the tomatoes, herbs, stock or wine, bring up to just simmering and cook gently for about 6 minutes. Season to taste with salt and pepper. Add the fish and cook for 2 minutes, taking care not to break up the fish as you gently stir around. Transfer to a lightly buttered pie or baking dish.

Fish Cobbler (above) and Fish Pie (above)

To make the topping, sift together the flours, baking powder and salt then rub in the butter. Add the herbs and paprika. Form into a light scone dough with the milk, and roll out on a floured board and cut out scones with a cutter (or use the rim of a glass tumbler). Arrange the scones in an overlapping ring around the edge of the dish and brush with a little milk. Sprinkle the cheese over the exposed centre of the dish and bake in a hot oven (220c, 425f, gas 7) for 15 minutes or until the scones have risen and browned.

You can prepare this dish in advance, making the scone topping just before cooking. SERVES 6

FISH PIE

Illustrated opposite

This is a very simple pie. I like to use smoked haddock for this but you could use a mixture of firm white fish such as cod or coley and mix it with half the amount of smoked haddock.

450 g / 1 lb potatoes
50 g / 2 oz butter
100 g / 4 oz mushrooms
450 g / 1 lb hot-smoked haddock fillets, skinned
and flaked
1 (227-g / 8-oz) can chopped tomatoes
150 ml / ¼ pint soured cream
50 g / 2 oz Cheddar cheese, grated

SCRUB the potatoes and leave on their skins. Boil the potatoes until just tender, about 15 minutes. Cool and cut them into chunky slices. Using a little of the butter, lightly grease a casserole or baking dish and arrange a layer of sliced potatoes on the base. Clean and slice the mushrooms.

Put the haddock, mushrooms and tomatoes with their juice into a bowl, add the soured cream and combine well. Tip this mixture on top of the potato layer, then arrange another layer of potato on top. Dot with scraps of butter and the grated cheese. Bake in a moderate oven (180c, 350f, gas 4) for 25 to 30 minutes. SERVES 4

BAKED PLAICE AND ORANGES

50 g/2 oz butter
900 g/2 lb plaice fillets
grated rind and juice of 1 lemon
salt and freshly ground black pepper
cayenne
2 oranges, peeled and sliced
watercress sprigs to garnish

LIGHTLY butter an ovenproof dish and place the plaice fillets on the bottom. Dot the fillets with the remaining butter and add the grated rind and juice of the lemon, making sure the surface of the fish is well coated. Season with salt and pepper and sprinkle with cayenne. Add the sliced oranges and bake in a moderately hot oven (200 c, 400 f, gas 6) for 10 to 15 minutes. Serve with the juices left from baking and garnish with sprigs of watercress. SERVES 4–6

PLAICE WITH SPICY MARINADE

4 medium plaice, cleaned
coriander leaves or parsley sprigs to garnish

MARINADE
150 g/5 oz natural yogurt
2 tablespoons concentrated tomato purée
2 cloves garlic, crushed
juice of ½ lemon
1 onion, finely chopped
1–2 teaspoons chilli powder, to taste
1 teaspoon coriander seeds, crushed
½ teaspoon ground turmeric
salt and freshly ground black pepper

PREPARE and wash the fish, pat dry, and cut slashes in a criss-cross pattern on both sides. Make the remaining ingredients into a paste, either in a food processor or blender, or by hand. Smother the fish all over with this marinade, making sure it penetrates all the slashes, and leave it in a cool place for about 2 to 3 hours.

Grill the fish under a moderate heat for 5 minutes on each side, brushing the plaice with the remaining paste occasionally. Transfer to warmed plates or a serving dish and dribble the juices from the grill pan over the fish, finishing with a garnish of coriander leaves or parsley. Plain boiled potatoes with chives, and a crisp green salad are good with this, and you could substitute megrim, witch or dab if plaice is not available. SERVES 4

SCAMPI PROVENÇALE

450 g/1 lb peeled scampi (Dublin Bay prawns)
court bouillon (page 169)
25 g/1 oz butter
1 small onion, finely chopped
1 clove garlic, crushed
450 g/1 lb tomatoes, peeled and chopped
(page 80)
1 tablespoon concentrated tomato purée
1 tablespoon chopped mixed herbs
2 tablespoons dry white wine (optional)
salt and freshly ground black pepper

POACH the scampi in the warm court bouillon for 5 to 7 minutes, then drain and keep warm.

Melt the butter in a saucepan and add the onion and garlic. Soften for a few minutes before adding the chopped tomato, tomato purée, herbs, wine (if using) and seasoning to taste. For a smooth sauce, blend in a liquidiser or food processor, or put through a sieve. Add the scampi to the sauce and heat through. Serve on a bed of plain boiled rice. SERVES 4

SALMON WITH THREE SAUCES

Illustrated on pages 110–11

1 (2-kg/4¼-lb) salmon, cleaned
salt and freshly ground pepper
50 g/2 oz butter, melted
lettuce to serve
cucumber and lemon slices to garnish

AVOCADO SAUCE
1 ripe avocado
150 ml/¼ pint natural yogurt
juice of ½–1 lemon

HORSERADISH SAUCE
1–2 tablespoons grated horseradish
150 ml/¼ pint soured cream
50 g/2 oz walnuts, chopped

COCKTAIL SAUCE
1–2 tablespoons tomato ketchup
150 ml/¼ pint mayonnaise (page 181)
a few drops of Tabasco sauce

WASH the salmon belly cavity, then pat dry with absorbent kitchen paper and season lightly. Grease a large sheet of aluminium foil with the melted butter. Place the salmon in a baking dish or tray and put in a cool oven (150C, 350F, gas 2). Bake for about 1 hour, remove from the oven and leave to cool.

Meanwhile, prepare the sauces. You can, of course, choose just one of the sauces to serve with your salmon, or, alternatively, make up all three and let your guests enjoy sampling them all.

For the avocado sauce, peel and stone the avocado, place in a food processor or blender and add the yogurt, a little salt and pepper, and lemon juice to taste. Blend until smooth.

For the horseradish sauce, mix the horseradish with the soured cream, add salt and pepper to taste, then mix in the walnuts.

For the cocktail sauce, mix the tomato ketchup with the mayonnaise and add Tabasco to taste.

Chill the sauces until ready to serve. Remove the salmon carefully from the foil and lay on a clean working surface or large chopping board. Using a long, thin-bladed sharp knife, cut through the skin along the length of the backbone, across tail and around head. Using the blade of the knife, peel off the skin and pull off the fins. With the back of the knife, scrape away the shallow layer of brown-coloured flesh over centre of fish. Turn the salmon over and repeat. Then cut down along the backbone of the fish, turn the knife flat and ease the fillet gently from the bone, and lift off. (This will have to be done in two pieces if it is a large fish.) At the head and tail, cut through the bone with kitchen scissors and peel away. Replace the upper fillet.

Prepare a bed of lettuce on a large serving dish and gently lift salmon into it. Garnish with thinly sliced cucumber and lemon. Keep cool until ready to serve. SERVES 8–10

HALIBUT IN VERMOUTH

1 onion, finely chopped
1 clove garlic, crushed
50 g/2 oz butter
675 g/1½ lb halibut fillets, skinned
and cubed (page 49)
about 150 ml/¼ pint dry vermouth
2 tablespoons fromage blanc or single cream
salt and freshly ground pepper
Hollandaise Sauce to serve (page 180)

SOFTEN the onion and garlic in the butter then add the cubed halibut. Continue cooking for 2 to 3 minutes before adding sufficient vermouth to cover the fish. Poach the halibut in the vermouth for about 5 minutes, then remove the halibut from the pan and keep warm. Reduce the cooking liquid by half and add the fromage blanc or cream. Season to taste and use the liquid to moisten the halibut. Serve with the hollandaise sauce. SERVES 4

Sole Véronique (page 112) and Skate in Orange and Cider Sauce (page 116); a simply poached salmon steak served with Three Sauces (above)

SOLE VÈRONIQUE

Illustrated on pages 110–11

8 sole fillets
1 onion, sliced
1 bay leaf
sprig of parsley
pinch each of salt and freshly ground black pepper
bones and trimmings from sole or 150 ml/¼ pint fish stock (page 170)
150–300 ml/¼–½ pint dry white wine
a small bunch of seedless grapes to garnish

SAUCE
25 g/1 oz flour
25 g/1 oz butter
150 ml/¼ pint milk
150 ml/¼ pint double cream

SKIN the fillets (see page 49), and place in a lightly buttered, ovenproof baking dish. Surround the fillets with the sliced onion, bay leaf, parsley, and a pinch of salt and freshly ground black pepper. You can also add the bones and trimmings from the sole to flavour the dish – or add the fish stock. Pour in the wine just to cover, and bake in a moderate oven (160c, 325f, gas 3) for 20 minutes, according to thickness of fillets. When cooked, transfer the fillets to a warmed serving dish, keep warm, and reduce the strained cooking liquid to 6 tablespoons.

In a saucepan, cook the flour in the melted butter over a gentle heat, and gradually stir in the milk and reduced stock. Check the seasoning and alter as necessary to taste. Remove from the heat and stir in the double cream. Coat your arrangement of fillets with this sauce, and garnish with the washed and dried grapes. Serve immediately with tiny new potatoes tossed in parsley. SERVES 4

SOLE WITH SOURED CREAM AND GHERKIN SAUCE

You can use witch, megrim or dab in place of the lemon sole in this recipe.

4 lemon sole fillets
salt and freshly ground black pepper
25 g/1 oz butter
150 ml/¼ pint soured cream
300 ml/½ pint fish stock (page 170)
2–3 gherkins, sliced

TRIM the fillets. season with salt and pepper to taste, and dot with butter. Then grill the fish under a moderate heat for about 5 minutes each side (according to the thickness of the fillets) – be careful not to overcook. Transfer to a warm serving dish, and keep hot. Combine the soured cream and fish stock, and heat carefully to just under boiling point. Add the sliced gherkins and cook gently for 1 minute. Pour the sauce over the fillets and serve immediately with plain boiled potatoes or fresh bread, and a simple crisp green salad. SERVES 2

SOLE À LA MEUNIÈRE

6–8 large sole fillets
100 g/4 oz flour
salt and freshly ground black pepper
150 ml/¼ pint milk
175 g/6 oz butter
juice of ½ lemon
2 tablespoons coarsely chopped fresh parsley
1 lemon, quartered, to garnish

RINSE and dry the fillets. Season the flour with salt and pepper. Dip the fillets in milk, drain and coat lightly in flour. Melt about 100 g/4 oz of the butter carefully in a heavy pan, taking care not to burn. Cook the fillets until golden brown on both sides. Place the fish on a hot serving dish and keep warm. Wipe out the pan and melt the remaining butter, cook to a golden brown. Immediately add the lemon juice and parsley, adjusting the seasoning if necessary. Pour over the fish and garnish with lemon wedges. SERVES 3–4

SOLE BONNE FEMME

4 shallots, chopped
100 g/4 oz mushrooms, sliced
75 g/3 oz butter
2 tablespoons parsley, chopped
900 g/2 lb sole fillets, halved lengthways and skinned (page 49)
salt and freshly ground black pepper
4 tablespoons dry white wine
150 ml/$\frac{1}{4}$ pint fish stock (page 170)
2 tablespoons lemon juice
25 g/1 oz flour
parsley sprigs and lemon twists to serve

SHALLOW fry the shallots and mushrooms in 50 g/2 oz butter. Add the parsley and spread on the base of an ovenproof dish. Roll up the sole fillets from head to tail, put into the casserole dish and season well. Pour over the wine, stock and lemon juice. Bake in a moderate oven (180 C, 350 F, gas 4) for 15 minutes.

Transfer the sole to a heated serving dish and thicken the liquid with beurre manie (25 g/1 oz butter kneaded with 25 g/1 oz flour to form a paste). Pour the sauce over the sole and serve hot, garnished with parsley sprigs and lemon twists. SERVES 4–6

PAPER-WRAPPED LEMON FILLETS

1 small onion, finely chopped
40 g/1$\frac{1}{2}$ oz butter
1 tablespoon chopped parsley
1 tablespoon chopped mixed herbs
squeeze of lemon juice
50 g/2 oz fresh breadcrumbs
ground ginger
salt and pepper
4 (225-g/8-oz) lemon sole or plaice fillets, skinned (page 49)
greaseproof paper

COOK the onion in 15 g/$\frac{1}{2}$ oz of the butter until soft but not brown. Add the parsley, mixed herbs, lemon juice and breadcrumbs.

Cut four 20 × 25-cm/8 × 10-in pieces of greaseproof paper and spread with the remaining butter. Sprinkle each lightly with the ginger, salt and pepper to taste. Place the fish on the paper and cover half with the breadcrumb mixture. Fold each fillet over and wrap securely in the paper, twisting the ends tightly. Bake in a moderately hot oven (200 C, 400 F, gas 6) for 15 minutes and serve in crisp, brown individual wraps. SERVES 4

PAELLA

Illustrated opposite

Although there are endless variations of this dish, I have omitted one ingredient that should always be included in a classic paella – MEAT! I personally prefer the unadulterated taste of shellfish and fish.

1.75 litres/3 pints mussels
1 medium cooked lobster or 225 g/8 oz monkfish
350 g/12 oz prepared squid
12 scallops
1 red pepper, deseeded
1 green pepper, deseeded
6 tablespoons olive oil
2 large Spanish onions, finely chopped
900 g/2 lb basmati rice
150 ml/¼ pint dry white wine
1 litre/1¾ pints fish stock (page 170)
2–3 teaspoons saffron powder
2 bay leaves
225 g/8 oz frozen petit pois
450 g/1 lb peeled cooked prawns
salt and freshly ground black pepper

GARNISH
8 unshelled cooked prawns
lemon wedges

PREPARE the mussels as described on page 56, and cook in a little water in a large pan until they have opened. Remember to throw away any that have not opened. Reserve the cooking liquid. Shell the lobster (see page 50), or skin and bone the monkfish (see page 48) and cut up the meat. Slice the squid into thin rings and slice the scallops. Slice the red and green peppers into thin strips and gently cook in 2 tablespoons of the olive oil. Remove from the pan and keep warm. Add the sliced squid and scallops (and monkfish if used) to the pan and turn them gently as they cook, then remove and keep warm. In a large paella dish or shallow pan, gently cook the finely chopped onion in the remaining olive oil until transparent. Add the rice and fry gently for a few more minutes, then pour in the wine, fish stock and reserved mussel stock. Bring up to simmering point, then add the saffron powder and give a few careful stirs; add the bay leaves at this stage. After about 10 to 15 minutes the rice, now a lovely saffron yellow, should have taken up the stock quite nicely, and you can stir in the petit pois. Add the prawns, all the reserved fish, the mussels and the red and green pepper, and, again, give a few gentle stirs. Let all heat through, taste and season with salt and pepper accordingly. Garnish with whole unshelled prawns, and wedges of lemon. Traditionally, paella is eaten with a spoon. Do not forget to remove the bay leaves just before serving. SERVES 8

SEAFOOD PANCAKES

Illustrated opposite

100 g/4 oz plain flour
pinch of salt
1 egg
300 ml/½ pint milk
225 g/8 oz cooked white fish fillets, skinned and cut into chunks
225 g/8 oz peeled cooked prawns
1 quantity Mornay Sauce (page 173)
a little oil or butter

TO SERVE (optional)
½ quantity Watercress Sauce (page 176)
lemon wedges

MIX together the flour and salt, make a well in the centre and add the egg and half the milk. Gradually work in the flour and beat until smooth. Add the remaining liquid gradually and stir well. Leave this mixture to stand.

Meanwhile, stir the white fish and prawns into the mornay sauce. Heat the oil or butter in a frying pan and make the pancakes from the reserved batter. Make the pancakes into cones and fill with the sauce. Serve with the watercress sauce, if using, or serve plain with lemon wedges. SERVES 4–6

Paella (above) and Seafood Pancakes (above)

SKATE WITH BLACK BUTTER

The butter is not black at all in this dish, just melted over a medium heat until it turns a sizzling deep golden colour. Have all the ingredients ready as the success of this dish depends on cooking it quickly and serving immediately. Plain boiled potatoes are good with this dish to soak up the delicious juices and butter.

675 g/1½ lb skate wings, cut into wedges
600 ml/1 pint court bouillon (page 169) or
white wine and water
about 100 g/4 oz butter
juice of 1 lemon or wine vinegar
1 tablespoon chopped parsley
1–2 tablespoons capers

POACH the skate wings in the warm court bouillon as described on page 25. Transfer to a warm serving dish and keep warm. Melt the butter in a pan until it turns a sizzling deep golden and pour over the fish. Put the lemon juice or wine vinegar into the pan and stir furiously for about 20 seconds and pour this over the fish as well, then scatter over the chopped parsley and capers. SERVES 4

SKATE IN ORANGE AND CIDER SAUCE

—————— *Illustrated on pages 110–11* ——————

4 skate wings
1 small onion, finely chopped
300 ml/½ pint dry cider
juice and rind of 1 orange
salt and freshly ground black pepper
capers
squeeze of lemon juice
4 tablespoons double cream or fromage blanc
orange peel and lemon wedges to garnish

PLACE the skate wings in a large shallow pan. Add the onion, cider, orange juice and a piece of thinly pared rind, then a pinch of salt and pepper. Bring slowly up to barely simmering, and poach for about 15 minutes. Lift the skate wings out, and keep them on a warmed serving dish. Turn up the heat, add the capers and boil the cooking liquid until it is reduced and thick, then check the seasoning. Add a squeeze of lemon juice, remove from the heat and swirl in the cream or fromage blanc. Pour the sauce over the skate wings and serve immediately, garnished with thinly pared ribbons of orange peel and wedges of lemon. Alternatively, thinly slice a lemon and quarter the slices to form a garnish. SERVES 4

TROUT BAKED IN RED WINE

4 trout, cleaned
1 large onion, thinly sliced
1 large carrot, thinly sliced
2 tablespoons chopped parsley
1 bay leaf
salt and freshly ground black pepper
300 ml/½ pint red wine
1 teaspoon anchovy essence
50 g/2 oz butter (optional)
1 tablespoon chopped parsley to garnish

PLACE the trout in a buttered ovenproof dish, on a layer of the vegetables and herbs, season well and top with another layer. Pour over the wine and bake, covered with a lid or aluminium foil, in a moderately hot oven (190C, 375F, gas 5) for 20 to 25 minutes. Remove the trout and boil up the juices and vegetables until well reduced. Add the anchovy essence and butter, if using, and strain over the fish. Garnish with chopped parsley. SERVES 4

TROUT WITH ALMONDS

Illustrated on page 51

flour for coating
salt and freshly ground black pepper
4 medium trout, cleaned
100 g / 4 oz butter
100 g / 4 oz flaked almonds
juice of $\frac{1}{2}$ lemon
fennel sprigs and lemon twists to garnish
(optional)

SEASON the flour with salt and pepper and dust the trout. Fry in half the butter for 3 to 4 minutes on each side. Remove and add the rest of the butter to the pan with the almonds. Fry gently until golden, add the lemon juice and a little seasoning to taste, then heat through before pouring over the trout. Garnish with sprigs of fennel and twists of lemon. SERVES 4

TROUT TANDOORI

This dish is nice with boiled rice mixed with peas and chopped parsley.

4 small to medium trout, cleaned
lemon wedges to garnish

MARINADE
1 clove garlic, crushed
1 (2.5-cm / 1-in) piece fresh root ginger, finely grated
2 tablespoons lemon juice
150 ml / $\frac{1}{4}$ pint natural yogurt
1 tablespoon ground coriander
1 tablespoon ground cumin
$\frac{1}{2}$ teaspoon allspice
1 teaspoon garam masala
pinch of cayenne
generous pinch of freshly ground black pepper
a few drops of yellow and red food colouring
(optional)

COMBINE all the marinade ingredients. Take care if adding the food colouring not to overdo it. Make three or four slashes in each side of the fish and cover with the marinade, making sure it penetrates the slashes. Leave the trout to marinate in a glass dish for 3 hours in a cool place, covered with cling film. Bake in a hot oven (220 C, 425 F, gas 7), uncovered, basting frequently, for about 20 minutes, or until the flesh is tender. Garnish with lemon wedges. SERVES 4

SIMPLE FISH CURRY

450 g / 1 lb patna rice
675–900 g / 1 $\frac{1}{2}$–2 lb coley, cod, hake or pollock fillets
50 g / 2 oz butter
1 medium onion, finely sliced
$\frac{1}{2}$ teaspoon cayenne
2 apples, cored and diced
2 tablespoons fish stock (page 170) or white wine
1 tablespoon mango chutney
1 quantity Mild Curry Sauce (page 173)

COOK the rice in boiling water, drain and keep warm on a serving dish.

Skin the fish (see page 49) and cut into bite-sized pieces. Melt the butter in a heavy pan, and soften the onion with the cayenne over a gentle heat. Add the apple and fish then sauté for a few minutes. Add the wine or stock and mango chutney, and stir over the heat for 2 to 3 minutes. Remove from the heat. Reheat the curry sauce in a separate saucepan, and add the fish, apple and onion, scraping up all the wine and pan juices. Carefully stir over a gentle heat and pour over the serving dish or rice. SERVES 6–8

TURBOT AND LEMON AU GRATIN

Turbot is a fish of exceptional flavour. It is such a lovely fish that simply poaching or baking the fillets with the addition of a savoury butter would normally be quite enough. However, try this recipe for a change.

4 turbot steaks or fillets, about 2.5 cm/1 in thick
250 ml/8 fl oz fish stock (page 170)
a little butter
4 tablespoons mayonnaise (page 181)
6 tablespoons fromage blanc or natural yogurt
juice of ½ lemon
salt and freshly ground black pepper
75 g/3 oz Cheddar cheese, grated
2–3 tablespoons breadcrumbs

POACH the turbot in the fish stock (see page 25). Using a slotted spoon, transfer to a lightly buttered gratin or baking dish. Combine the mayonnaise, fromage blanc or natural yogurt, lemon juice, pinch each of salt and pepper, and 1 to 2 tablespoons of the cooking liquid. Pour over the fillets, and sprinkle over the grated cheese and breadcrumbs. Brown under the grill, or in the oven, and take to the table to serve straight away with sautéd potatoes and whole green beans. Alternatively, serve as below with grilled tomatoes and mushrooms on a base of endive or crisp lettuce. SERVES 4

WHITING IN TOMATO AND BASIL SAUCE

salt and freshly ground black pepper
4 whiting fillets
12 bruised leaves of basil
3–4 tablespoons dry white wine
fresh basil or watercress to garnish

SAUCE
1 tablespoon olive oil
25 g/1 oz butter
1 small onion, very finely chopped
1 carrot, grated
6 ripe tomatoes, peeled, deseeded and
chopped (page 80)
2 teaspoons concentrated tomato purée
½ teaspoon brown sugar
2 tablespoons fresh chopped basil
fromage blanc or soured cream
squeeze of lemon juice

SEASON the fillets, place in an aluminium foil parcel and, before sealing, cover with the bruised leaves of basil and splash in the wine. Set in a steamer (see page 26) and, when cooked, transfer to a warmed serving dish, keep warm and reserve the juices.

Heat up the olive oil and butter in a heavy saucepan, soften down the finely chopped onion and grated carrot for 5 minutes, stirring and not allowing to brown. Add the tomatoes, tomato purée, sugar, basil and the reserved cooking juices from the whiting and cook over a very low heat until all is tender. Put this sauce into a food processor or blender and purée until smooth, return to the pan and reheat. Add the fromage blanc or soured cream, season, check for taste and sharpen up with a squeeze of fresh lemon juice. Arrange the sauce and fillets on a warmed serving dish with leaves of basil or watercress to garnish, and serve. SERVES 4

FISH, COURGETTE AND BROWN RICE BAKE

I have to say that this was an invention of 'left-overs' but, since its inauguration in my home, has become a useful standard meal. This pie is really scrumptious. I like to let the pie settle for a few minutes before serving with hot, freshly cooked green vegetables.

4–6 courgettes
450–675 g / 1–1½ lb white fish fillets
salt and freshly ground black pepper
4 tomatoes, peeled and sliced (page 80)
1 onion, finely chopped
2 cloves garlic, crushed
2 tablespoons sunflower oil
450 g / 1 lb cooked brown rice
1 bunch parsley, chopped
4 tablespoons chopped fresh herbs, as available
50 g / 2 oz Cheddar cheese, grated (optional)

SAUCE
25 g / 1 oz unsalted butter
25 g / 1 oz flour
300 ml / ½ pint milk
50 g / 2 oz cheese, grated
1 egg (optional)

LIGHTLY butter a baking dish. Thinly slice the courgettes and arrange over the base and up the sides of the dish. Slice the fillets into thick strips and pack into the dish – season with the salt and freshly ground black pepper. Cover with the slices of tomato. Soften the onion and crushed garlic in the sunflower oil. Mix into the cooked brown rice and add all the herbs. Top the pie with this mixture. Make a sauce with the butter, flour, milk, cheese, and, if liked, thicken a little more with the egg. Pour over the top of the pie and bake in a moderately hot oven (200 c, 400 f, gas 6) for 30 minutes. (I usually top the pie with a handful of grated cheese before baking.) SERVES 4

ITALIAN FISH BAKE

25 g / 1 oz butter
1 clove garlic, crushed
350 g / 12 oz courgettes, sliced
1 onion, sliced
1 red pepper, deseeded and sliced
100 g / 4 oz mushrooms, sliced
1 tablespoon chopped fresh or 1 teaspoon dried mixed herbs
4 medium red mullet or snappers
salt and freshly ground black pepper
25 g / 1 oz fresh breadcrumbs

MELT the butter and add the garlic, vegetables and herbs. Gently cook for 5 minutes. Using a sharp knife, split the fish along the belly and clean (see page 44). Snip off the fins and wash the fish well. Keep whole. Place the fish on individual pieces of aluminium foil then season with salt and freshly ground black pepper. Arrange the vegetables around each fish and fold over the foil to make a parcel, then seal completely. Bake in a moderately hot oven (190 c, 375 f, gas 5) for 30 minutes. Open each parcel and sprinkle the breadcrumbs over the fish. Bake for a further 10 minutes until the breadcrumbs are crisp. Serve with boiled new potatoes. SERVES 4

SEAFOOD RING

Illustrated on pages 54–5

4 plaice fillets
4 smoked haddock fillets
225 g/8 oz white fish fillets
50 g/2 oz diced red and green peppers
25 g/1 oz sweetcorn
salt and pepper
2 tablespoons single cream
1 egg white, stiffly beaten

SKIN the fish fillets as shown on page 49 then cut in half lengthways, to form quarter-cut fillets. Using alternative coloured fillets, line a 1.15-litres/2-pints ring mould with the plaice and haddock fillets – do not worry if they overlap the sides.

Pound the white fish fillets until smooth, add the vegetables and seasoning. Stir in the cream and fold in the egg white. Spoon into the mould and fold the fillets over to cover the filling. Cover with aluminium foil. Place in a pan half-filled with water. Cover, bring to the boil, and simmer for 20 minutes. Remove and stand for several minutes to set. Turn out onto a plate and chill before serving with a mixed salad. SERVES 6

SEAFOOD DIANA

25 g/1 oz butter
50 g/2 oz flour
150 ml/¼ pint milk
3 tablespoons dry vermouth
100 g/4 oz peeled cooked prawns
100 g/4 oz scampi
100 g/4 oz white fish fillets, skinned and chopped (page 49)
100 g/4 oz mushrooms, finely chopped
1 teaspoon lemon juice
rind of ½ lemon
salt and freshly ground black pepper
350 g/12 oz puff pastry, defrosted if frozen
1 egg, beaten, to glaze

MELT the butter and stir in the flour. Gradually add the milk, whisking con-tinuously until smooth (the sauce is quite thick). Add 2 tablespoons of the vermouth and all the other filling ingredients, including seasoning to taste. Bring to the boil; simmer for 8 minutes, stirring occasionally. Spoon into a bowl and cool slightly. Stir in the remaining vermouth. Cover with cling film and refrigerate until very cold. Roll out the pastry and cut into eight 13-cm/5-in squares. Spoon the fish mixture onto the squares, dampen the edges of the pastry and fold over to form a triangle. Seal well and glaze with the beaten egg.

Bake the triangles in a hot oven (220c, 425f, gas 7) for 25 minutes. SERVES 4

GRILLED FISH WITH PESTO

Illustrated on page 7

4 whole plaice, red mullet, or cutlets of cod, hake, pollack, etc.

PESTO
2 large cloves garlic, coarsely chopped
2 tablespoons pine nuts
pinch each of salt and freshly ground black pepper
1 large bunch fresh basil, finely chopped
4 tablespoons freshly grated Parmesan
300 ml/½ pint olive oil
2 tablespoons water

PUT the pesto ingredients into a food processor or blender and purée until the mixture is smooth. Or, in a pestle and mortar, pound together the garlic, add the pine nuts, salt, pepper and basil. Transfer the mixture to a bowl and slowly add the oil, stirring all the time, finishing with the water.

Cook the fish under a pre-heated grill until tender but still firm. Remove to a warmed serving dish or plates, and put 1 to 2 tablespoons of pesto over each fish. Serve immediately with a fresh green salad and warm fresh white bread rolls to mop up the juices. SERVES 4

MIXED SHELLFISH WITH GREEN FETTUCINE

4 large or 6 medium scallops
2 prepared squid
2 tablespoons butter
1 medium onion, finely chopped
1 clove garlic, crushed
20 peeled cooked prawns
1 tablespoon finely chopped parsley
1 teaspoon finely chopped coriander leaves
150 ml/¼ pint dry white wine
150 ml/¼ pint natural yogurt
3 tablespoons double cream
salt and freshly ground black pepper
675 g/1½ lb green fettucine
4 unshelled cooked prawns to garnish
25 g/1 oz Parmesan cheese, freshly grated

PREPARE the scallops (see page 53) and slice the white flesh into three pieces. Reserve the corals. Slice the squid into 5-mm/¼-in strips.

Heat the butter in a large, heavy frying pan or wok then gently sauté the onion and garlic. Add the squid, and stir-fry for 4 minutes, then add the scallops and corals and cook for 2 minutes, stir-frying all the time. Add the prawns and continue cooking for 1 minute, then throw in the parsley and coriander and cook for 30 seconds, shaking the pan and stirring all the time. Add the wine, bring up to the boil and cook until all is slightly reduced. Remove from the heat and stir in the combined yogurt and double cream and season with a little pepper.

Meanwhile, cook the fettucine in plenty of boiling salted water (add a drop of oil to prevent it sticking). Drain well, heap onto a heated serving dish and fork in the shellfish mixture and sauce. Garnish with the whole unpeeled prawns and scatter over the Parmesan, then serve immediately. SERVES 6

MUSSELS WITH PASTA SHELLS

1.15 litres/2 pints fresh mussels
150 ml/¼ pint dry red wine
1 onion, finely chopped
2 cloves garlic, crushed
2 tablespoons olive oil
1–2 teaspoons oregano
1 (397-g/14-oz) can chopped tomatoes
50 g/2 oz concentrated tomato purée
salt and freshly ground black pepper
400 g/14 oz pasta shells
1 tablespoon chopped parsley to garnish
squeeze of lemon juice to serve

PREPARE the mussels (see page 56) and set in a large heavy pan with the wine and steam open. Cook for 5 minutes.

Soften the onion and garlic in the hot olive oil. Add the oregano, tomatoes and tomato purée, and wine liquid from the mussels, and cook until the sauce is thick and reduced somewhat. Season to taste with salt and pepper. Meanwhile, cook the pasta in lots of boiling salted water, into which you have added a drop of oil to prevent the pasta sticking. Fresh pasta takes 2 or 3 minutes to cook – but dried will take about 12 minutes and should be *al dente* (with a firm bite). Put the drained pasta into a large warmed serving dish and stir in the sauce, and mussels, in their shells. Garnish with chopped parsley and squeeze a little fresh lemon juice over.
Important reminder: any mussels which have not opened during cooking must be discarded. SERVES 4

FISH FONDUE

Illustrated on page 22

Fish fondue, or raw fish dipped in simmering stock, is a popular Japanese and Chinese method of enjoying fish and is wonderfully suited to the naturally tender flesh of fish. Use a selection of really fresh, firm-fleshed fish or shellfish, according to taste and availability. You do not need to use a proper fondue pot – a saucepan will do, set on a trivet over a spirit burner.

675–900 g/ 1½–2 lb firm-fleshed white fish and shellfish such as cod, halibut, scallops, prawns or scampi
well-flavoured court bouillon or fish stock
(pages 169 and 170)

SALAD SUGGESTIONS
grated carrot and chopped mint
fresh beetroot sprinkled with snipped chives
orange and watercress
potato and onion
shredded lettuce and spring onion
brown rice with mixed chopped nuts and chopped parsley

SAUCES
soy sauce
Tartare Sauce (page 182)
Cold Tomato Sauce (page 177)
savoury butters (page 184)
Apple and Horseradish Sauce (page 179)

PREPARE the fish according to type and slice the fish and shellfish into thin slices. Place in attractive bowls or on plates and surround with bowls of salad and the various sauces or dips. Provide each guest with fondue forks and let them help themselves to salad. People can then spear pieces of fish on the fork and immerse them in the simmering stock for a few minutes. The fish can be dipped in the sauce of their choice. SERVES 4–6

CRISPY FISH HOTPOT

This dish goes well with chunky sautéd potatoes and whole green beans.

350 g/ 12 oz courgettes, thinly sliced
2 red dessert apples, cored and thinly sliced
1 large onion, sliced
1 teaspoon dried sage
675 g/ 1½ lb huss fillets, cut into small chunks
salt and pepper
1 teaspoon mustard powder
50 g/ 2 oz fresh breadcrumbs
25 g/ 1 oz butter

LAYER a greased ovenproof dish with the courgettes, apple and onion. Sprinkle with the sage, cover and bake in a moderately hot oven (190C, 375F, gas 5) for 30 minutes. Remove from the oven, place the fish on top and season. Mix together the mustard powder and breadcrumbs and sprinkle over the fish. Dot with the butter and bake for another 25 minutes. SERVES 4–6

A SIMPLE SAUTÉ OF LOBSTER OR CRAWFISH

Lobster and crawfish are generally an occasional treat for fish lovers, and I think that the best way to sample this exceptional seafood is simply and with the minimum fuss: with a good salad and home-made mayonnaise or dressing. I find many of the classic cooked shellfish recipes overwhelmingly rich. However, this recipe avoids the usual rich sauces associated with shellfish – and yet there is still that special and exotic flavour and taste.

1 cooked lobster or crawfish
1 clove garlic, crushed (optional)
50 g / 2 oz butter
2 tablespoons dry sherry
2 tablespoons double cream
salt and freshly ground black pepper
2 tablespoons chopped parsley

EXTRACT the meat from the lobster (see page 50). Cut all the flesh into bite-sized pieces. If using garlic, soften it in the melted butter in a heavy pan then quickly add the cubes of lobster meat. Sauté them gently for about 3 minutes, turning them carefully so they cook evenly. Then pour in the dry sherry, continue to cook for 30 seconds, remove from the heat and swirl in the double cream. Season to taste with salt and pepper. Sprinkle with finely chopped parsley and take the pan to the table to serve. This dish goes well with plain parsleyed new potatoes and a simple crisp green salad. A bowl of hot rice with chopped parsley would also be good to offset the richness of the lobster. SERVES 2–3

STUFFED SQUID WITH TOMATO SAUCE

———— *Illustrated on pages 174–5* ————

900 g / 2 lb squid
olive oil for frying

STUFFING
100 g / 4 oz wholemeal breadcrumbs
1 large onion, finely chopped
2 tablespoons chopped fresh green herbs, as available
1 clove garlic, finely chopped (optional)
100 g / 4 oz blanched almonds
chopped reserved tentacles of the squid
salt and freshly ground black pepper
1 egg, beaten

SAUCE
1 (397-g / 14-oz) can chopped tomatoes
150 ml / $\frac{1}{4}$ pint dry white wine
1 onion, finely chopped
2 tablespoons chopped parsley
salt and pepper

PREPARE the squid (see page 56) or ask your fishmonger to prepare them (they are often available already prepared). Combine the stuffing ingredients to make a nice moist mixture, stuff the sacs and sew up with a trussing needle and kitchen string. Heat up the olive oil and turn the stuffed squid in the pan until browned all over. Mix together the sauce ingredients, combining well. Place the stuffed squid in a casserole dish, and pour over the blended ingredients of the sauce. Cover tightly and bake in a cool oven (150 c, 300 f, gas 2) for $1\frac{1}{2}$ hours. Serve hot. (Incidentally, this dish is also very good chilled with crisp green salad.) SERVES 4–6

STIR-FRIED SQUID

This dish goes well with pasta, especially thin noodles or spaghetti. For extra flavour, toss the cooked pasta in the pan juices just before serving.

450 g / 1 lb squid
3 tablespoons oil
6 spring onions, sliced, with all green parts included
1 head celery, finely sliced
1 tablespoon finely chopped fresh root ginger
salt and freshly ground black pepper
1–2 tablespoons rice wine (sake) or sherry
lemon wedges to serve

PREPARE the squid as illustrated on page 56 or buy it prepared from the fishmonger. Slice the sac into 5-mm/¼-in rings and cut the tentacles in half.

Heat the oil in a wok or very large, heavy frying pan. Drop in the squid and stir-fry for 2 minutes, then add the spring onions, celery and ginger and continue for 1 to 1½ minutes, stir-frying all the time. Season with salt and pepper, and throw in the rice wine or sherry, stirring all the time. Serve immediately, garnished with lemon wedges. SERVES 2–3

NOTE: You can add extra, crunchy vegetables to this stir-fry. Try strips of red or green pepper or shredded Chinese Cabbage.

LOBSTER THERMIDOR

A gourmet dish for special occasions.

2 (675-g/1½-lb) lobsters
75 g/3 oz butter
1 shallot, finely chopped
50 g/2 oz flour
4 tablespoons dry white wine
300 ml/½ pint fish stock (page 170)
1 teaspoon prepared English mustard
salt and freshly ground pepper
juice of ½ lemon (optional)
4 tablespoons wholemeal breadcrumbs,
browned in a little butter
1 tablespoon chopped parsley

COOK the lobsters as described on page 32, if they are not already cooked. Open out the lobster back-side down and, with a strong sharp knife, cut in half lengthways, taking care not to damage the shell. Extract the meat from the body and claws, as described on page 50. Reserve the lobster shells and oil lightly.

Chop up the lobster meat, and gently sauté in 25 g/1 oz of the butter for 4 minutes, turning all the time, then set aside. Melt the remaining butter in a saucepan and gently cook the very finely chopped shallot, then add the flour and cook for 1 to 2 minutes. Gradually stir in the wine and fish stock to make a thick sauce, then add the mustard, salt and pepper to taste, and a little lemon juice, if desired. Fold the lobster meat into this sauce, and pour into the lightly oiled lobster shells. Sprinkle the browned breadcrumbs over the mixture in the shells, and brown under a hot grill until golden and bubbling. Sprinkle with the chopped parsley and serve immediately with really fresh bread and a crisp green salad. SERVES 4

FISH PIE WITH CRUNCHY TOPPING

A rather sweet and delicate dish which is delicious served with broccoli and a chilled German white wine.

675 g/1½ lb white fish fillets (e.g. haddock or cod), skinned (page 49)
300 ml/½ pint Béchamel Sauce (page 172)
50 g/2 oz cheese, grated
pinch each of nutmeg and ground rosemary or very finely chopped fresh rosemary
100 g/4 oz pine nuts
100 g/4 oz wholemeal breadcrumbs
25 g/1 oz butter

CUT the fish fillets into small pieces and add to the warm and slightly thick sauce. Stir in the grated cheese and add nutmeg and rosemary to taste. Lightly butter a shallow gratin dish and pour in the mixture. Scatter over the pine nuts then cover with breadcrumbs. Dot with tiny nuts of the butter and bake in a hot oven (220 c, 425 f, gas 7) for 15 to 20 minutes, until the topping is really crunchy. SERVES 4

DEVILLED CRAB

350 g/12 oz crab meat
1 teaspoon French mustard
2 teaspoons Worcestershire sauce
juice of ½ lemon
pinch each of salt, freshly ground pepper and cayenne
150 ml/¼ pint natural yogurt
2 tablespoons fresh wholemeal breadcrumbs
50 g/2 oz Parmesan cheese, grated (optional)
a little butter
lemon wedges to garnish
watercress salad to serve

EXTRACT the meat from the crab (see page 52). Flake the white meat, and combine with the brown meat (cream) in a small mixing bowl. Add the mustard, Worcestershire sauce, lemon juice, salt, pepper, cayenne and yogurt.

Pile the mixture into lightly oiled crab or scallop shells. Scatter with the breadcrumbs and Parmesan cheese, if using. Dot with tiny scraps of butter and bake in a moderate oven (180 c, 350 f, gas 4) or under a grill for 10 to 15 minutes, until golden. Garnish with wedges of lemon and serve with a watercress salad. SERVES 2–3

CATFISH PIE

675 g/1½ lb catfish fillets, skinned
300 ml/½ pint cider
bouquet of fresh herbs (parsley, thyme, bayleaf)
salt and freshly ground black pepper
about 300 ml/½ pint white sauce (page 172)
450 g/1 lb potatoes, diced
2 cloves garlic, crushed (optional)
2 medium leeks, finely chopped
100 g/4 oz mushrooms, thinly sliced
1 quantity shortcrust pastry (page 62)
1 egg, beaten, to glaze

COOK the catfish in the cider with the bouquet of herbs and seasoning to taste for 10 minutes. Remove with a slotted spoon and flake the flesh, removing any bones. Cook the diced potato in the fish liquid until just tender. Drain and reserve. Add all the cooking liquid to the white sauce and stir in the garlic, if using.

Arrange the chopped leeks and mushrooms in the base of a lightly greased 1.25 litres/2 pints pie dish. Top the vegetables with the fish and potato, season lightly to taste and pour over the sauce. Roll out the pastry to make a lid and use to top the pie. Decorate, if liked, with pastry trimmings and glaze with the beaten egg. Bake in a hot oven (220 c, 425 f, gas 7) for 10 minutes then reduce to moderate (180 c, 350 f, gas 4) for a further 20 minutes. SERVES 6

MEDITERRANEAN FISH STEW

This is a very substantial dish and suitable for entertaining.

675 g/1½ lb white fish fillets
2 onions, chopped
2 cloves garlic, crushed
2–3 tablespoons olive oil
2 sticks celery, chopped
1 large green pepper, deseeded and chopped
1 large red pepper, deseeded and chopped
1 (397-g/14-oz) can chopped tomatoes
100 g/4 oz black olives, stoned
1 tablespoon fresh chopped herbs, as available
150 ml/¼ pint fish stock (page 170)
150 ml/¼ pint red wine
salt and freshly ground black pepper
175 g/6 oz peeled cooked prawns
2–3 tablespoons double cream, natural yogurt or fromage blanc
dash of Tabasco sauce (optional)
snipped chives to garnish

PREPARE the fish by skinning and trimming as necessary, then cut into bite-sized chunks.

Soften the onion and garlic in the olive oil then add the chopped vegetables, the olives and the herbs. Cook gently for about 5 minutes then add the fish stock and wine. Season to taste then add the fish, putting in the firmer-fleshed fish first, then the softer-fleshed fish and prawns. Cover and simmer for 10 minutes.

Remove from the heat and swirl in the double cream, yogurt or fromage blanc. Add the Tabasco sauce, if using. Sprinkle with the snipped chives and serve immediately with plain boiled potatoes or slices of French bread. SERVES 6–8

REALLY GOOD FISH AND CHIPS

A super British tradition when cooked well with good oil and fresh fish. And who can resist the occasional plate of fish and chips?

Here the chips can be oven baked, and the fish shallow fried – thus avoiding the smell and fuss usually associated with deep fried food.

450–675 g/1–1½ lb potatoes
sunflower oil
4 (225-g/8-oz) hake, cod or coley fillets
1 quantity batter (see page 185)

SCRUB the potatoes (you do not have to peel), and cut into slender chips. Rinse with cold water, drain and pat dry with absorbent kitchen paper or tea-towels. Put 1 or 2 tablespoons of oil into a polythene bag with the chips and shake them all around until they are evenly coated. (This could also be done in a basin with your fingers.) Spread the chips evenly on a large baking tray and put into the top of a hot oven (230 c, 450 F, gas 8) for about 50 to 55 minutes, turning over once halfway through the cooking time.

Meanwhile, trim, wash and pat dry the fish fillets and coat each one in batter (you could alternatively dip them in milk or beaten egg and coat them in seasoned breadcrumbs). Shallow fry in hot oil to seal, then turn down the heat slightly and continue to cook for a few minutes on each side.

Alternatively, you can deep fry the chips in hot oil (190 c/375 F) for 7 to 10 minutes until golden and crisp. The fish fillets can also be deep fried after coating with batter.

Dish up the fish and chips straight away on warmed plates with brown vinegar, tomato ketchup, or any of your favourite relishes. SERVES 4

Salads

Salad days can be winter or summer days. It is sad to think that few people realise how the huge variety of fish and shellfish available in this country can be combined with all manner of ingredients – simple or exotic – to produce wonderful salad dishes.

Try serving warm salads – for instance, pasta tossed in a good home-made vinaigrette with a selection of shellfish and heaped onto a bed of crisp lettuce is astonishingly simple and tasty. The judicious use of fresh herbs, cold firm white fish (cod, haddock, monkfish, etc.) tossed into a cocktail of chopped peppers, cold rice and topped with a mayonnaise or cocktail sauce makes a most acceptable starter or main course salad.

Let yourself be tempted by artichoke hearts, mange-tout, endive, radiccio, and all those special vegetables that we see increasingly on market stalls and supermarket shelves – they will all make a perfect marriage with the tender and succulent flesh of seafood. Even the simplest of presentations can be a visual delight. Dreamier still can be the delicate colours, textures and combinations of fish and shellfish used in a grand *fruits de mer* (or seafood platter). I think, perhaps, that salads offer the greatest scope for lovers of fish – do enjoy the recipes in this chapter, and use the Sauces and Dressings chapter to create your variations.

Monkfish and Avocado Salad (page 132) and
Kipper, Apple and Onion Salad (page 132)

MONKFISH AND AVOCADO SALAD

Illustrated on page 130

675 g/1½ lb monkfish, skinned and boned
(page 48)
300 ml/½ pint fish stock (page 170) or
dry white wine
4 courgettes, grated or shredded
2 ripe avocados, peeled and sliced
squeeze of lemon juice
2 sticks celery, very finely sliced
225 g/8 oz seedless white grapes
4 tablespoons mayonnaise (page 181)
4 tablespoons fromage blanc or natural yogurt
3–4 teaspoons concentrated tomato purée
pinch of cayenne

CUT the monkfish into medallions and poach in the stock or wine. Transfer with a slotted spoon to a cool dish or plate and set aside. Reserve 1 tablespoon of the cooking liquid for the sauce, and reserve the remaining liquid for a soup or stew – it can even be frozen for future use.

On a large oval or round serving plate or platter, make a border around the rim with the grated courgettes, then inside this circle arrange another circle of overlapping avocado slices. Sprinkle with lemon juice.

In a bowl, combine the monkfish, finely sliced celery and grapes. Mix together the mayonnaise, fromage blanc, tomato purée, cayenne and add a tiny squeeze of lemon juice to sharpen. Stir in 1 tablespoon of the cooled cooking liquid to thin down the sauce and add flavour.

Heap the fish, celery and grape mixture in the centre of the salad arrangement and pour the sauce all over.

The delicate shades of pale pink and pale green make this an elegant presentation for this summer salad. Keep it simple – a plate of thinly sliced fresh tomatoes on the side would be lovely – also fresh bread rolls. SERVES 4–6

KIPPER, APPLE AND ONION SALAD

Illustrated on page 130

225 g/8 oz cooked kipper fillets
2 dessert apples
1 small onion
4 tablespoons double cream
4 tablespoons natural yogurt
squeeze of lemon juice
salt and freshly ground black pepper
Chinese leaves to serve
parsley sprigs and lemon wedges to garnish

SKIN the kipper fillets, and cut into strips about 5 mm/¼ in thick and about 3 to 5 cm/1½ to 2 in long. Core the apples (leaving the skin on) and cut into small chunks. Slice the onion into extremely thin half rounds. There should be more or less equal quantities of these three ingredients, but cut down a little on the onion if it is strong.

Combine the cream and yogurt together, add a squeeze of lemon juice to taste and season with salt and pepper. Mix into the kipper, apple and onion mixture. Arrange 4 large Chinese leaves on a platter, and heap the mixture into the cradle of each leaf. Put wedges of lemon in between each leaf and distribute sprigs of parsley around the dish. SERVES 2–3

SALAD MONTE CRISTO

Illustrated on pages 134–5

450 g/1 lb cod fillet, skinned and cubed
(page 49)
150 ml/¼ pint court bouillon (page 169)
2 dessert pears, cut into chunks
50 g/2 oz walnut pieces
1 bunch watercress or endive, roughly chopped
salt and freshly ground black pepper
lemon slices to garnish

DRESSING
1 clove garlic, crushed
1 tablespoon white wine vinegar
5 tablespoons olive oil
2 tablespoons finely chopped fresh tarragon

POACH the cod in the court bouillon for 4 to 5 minutes. Drain and chill. Mix together the chilled fish with the remaining ingredients.

To make the dressing, put all the ingredients in a screw-top jar and shake well. Pour over the salad and serve garnished with lemon slices. SERVES 4

ARBROATH SALAD

Illustrated on pages 134–5

2 Arbroath smokies
black pepper
4 spring onions, chopped
100 g/4 oz cooked rice
2 hard-boiled eggs, diced
1 stick celery, sliced
vinaigrette dressing (page 184)
1 tablespoon chopped parsley to garnish

REMOVE the skin from the fish and flake the flesh into a bowl. Season with black pepper. Add the spring onions, rice, egg and celery. Mix in sufficient dressing to coat the ingredients. Toss well and serve garnished with the chopped parsley. SERVES 2–4

HARICOT BEAN AND FISH SALAD

Illustrated on pages 134–5

Use any firm-fleshed white fish for this salad; whiting is particularly good. This salad goes well with rye bread or wholemeal rolls.

225 g/8 oz haricot beans
salt and freshly ground black pepper
vinaigrette dressing (page 184)
450 g/1 lb cooked white fish, flaked
1 shallot or 4 spring onions
2 apples
1 orange
2–3 tablespoons chopped fresh herbs, as
available
100 g/4 oz black olives, stoned
4 tomatoes, peeled and quartered (page 80)
2 sticks celery, finely sliced
1 crisp lettuce or watercress to serve

COVER the beans with water and soak overnight. Drain, cover again with water, then simmer for about 2 to 3 hours in a covered pan until tender. Drain, season with salt and pepper (do not add any salt until the beans have been cooked as otherwise they will become rather tough) and while the beans are still hot, toss them in the dressing.

Flake the fish, slice the shallot or spring onions, core the apples and chop into tiny chunks, leaving the skin on. Peel, segment and chop the orange, keeping the juice. Combine all the ingredients in a large bowl and check the seasoning. Arrange on a bed of crisp lettuce or watercress. SERVES 4–6

Haricot Bean and Fish Salad (above), Salad Monte Cristo (above) and Arbroath Salad (above)

SKATE SALAD WITH RUSSIAN DRESSING

2 skate wings
600 ml / 1 pint court bouillon (page 169)
1 lettuce, shredded
1 bunch watercress, trimmed
1 cucumber, diced
4 sticks celery, sliced
1 bunch spring onions, sliced lengthways,
including the green part
100 g / 4 oz button mushrooms, thinly sliced
chopped fresh herbs to garnish (optional)

DRESSING
175 ml / 6 fl oz tomato juice
4 tablespoons olive oil
4 tablespoons lemon juice
1 small onion, chopped
1 tablespoon honey
pinch of salt
1 teaspoon paprika
1 clove garlic

POACH the skate wings in the warm court bouillon (see page 25), remove from the pan and cool. Thoroughly drain the fish, remove the skin, and shred the flesh from the wings. Reserve the stock for another dish.

Make up a salad using the lettuce, watercress, cucumber, celery, spring onions and mushrooms.

Blend the ingredients for the dressing in a food processor or blender. Combine the shredded skate and salad ingredients and toss in the dressing. Serve the chilled salad in a salad bowl. Sprinkle over fresh herbs as available – for example, chopped chives.
SERVES 4–6

LOBSTER SALAD WITH TARRAGON SAUCE

Lobster is a treat but you need only a small one for this exquisite dish. You could use crawfish or monkfish (its lack of bones, firm texture and lovely taste make it an interesting alternative), and I have also used steaks of fresh salmon, poached in a good stock, with wonderful results.

1 (675-g / 1½-lb) lobster or crawfish
2 cucumbers
½ teaspoon salt
1 teaspoon sugar
1–2 tablespoons tarragon vinegar
100 g / 4 oz petit pois
200 g / 7 oz mayonnaise
200 g / 7 oz natural yogurt
2–3 sprigs fresh tarragon, chopped
about 6 tablespoons lobster or fish stock
(page 170)
1 crisp lettuce
tarragon sprigs to garnish

EXTRACT the meat from the lobster (see page 50). A lobster stock can be made by pounding the lobster shell and boiling it in about 600 ml / 1 pint salted water for 30 minutes – with a handful of fresh herbs. Of course, the stock will need straining before use.

Peel and deseed the cucumbers then slice into matchsticks. Toss them in a basin with a marinade of salt, sugar and tarragon vinegar and leave in a cool place for 1 hour. Cook the petit pois in boiling salted water for 2 to 3 minutes, drain and leave to cool. Combine the mayonnaise, yogurt and chopped fresh tarragon – then carefully stir in 6 tablespoons of lobster or fish stock, to make a good consistency.

Shred the lettuce and make a bed on a platter. Cut the lobster meat into chunky slices and pile on top of the lettuce. Mix the peas with the rinsed, drained cucumber and arrange around the edge of the dish. Pour over the sauce and garnish with sprigs of fresh tarragon. SERVES 4

SALMON IN ASPIC

Illustrated on page 182

For a special occasion – a wedding buffet or summer party – this is an impressive and delicious way to serve a whole salmon. You could also use this method on grey mullet, John Dory, salmon trout or trout (or on a serving dish of salmon cutlets or steaks). For this dish it is worth buying a really good, large salmon to make the time spent preparing the dish really worthwhile.

1 large salmon
court bouillon (page 169)
1 crisp lettuce or endive
300 ml/$\frac{1}{2}$ pint fish stock (page 170)
1 egg white and the egg shell
1 tablespoon dry sherry
15 g/$\frac{1}{2}$ oz powdered gelatine
1 bunch radishes, very thinly sliced
1 bunch fresh mint
mayonnaise to serve

POACH the salmon in a fish kettle in the warm court bouillon (see page 25). Remove from the heat and leave to cool. If you do not have a fish kettle you can place the salmon on a large sheet of lightly buttered aluminium foil, make a loose parcel around the fish and pour in the court bouillon. Bake in a moderately hot oven (190c, 375f, gas 5) for 15 minutes per 450 g/1 lb. A really large fish can be cut into two or three pieces and wrapped in separate pieces of foil. After cooling and skinning, the fish can be rejoined and the joins cleverly disguised with a garnish or sauce.

When the whole poached or baked salmon is cooked, the skin can be easily peeled off, leaving the skin on the head and tail.

To make the aspic coating, add 300 ml/$\frac{1}{2}$ pint of the salmon poaching liquid (court bouillon) to the fish stock and boil down hard to reduce by half. Take off the heat and whisk in the egg white and add the broken egg shell to the liquid. This will clarify the stock. Strain the liquid through a muslin cloth and add the sherry. Stir in the powdered gelatine and continue stirring until it has dissolved. Leave the mixture to cool, then spoon a thin layer of the aspic over the salmon. Chill and leave to set, then overlap the sliced radish down the backbone and arrange mint leaves decoratively along each side. Coat the salmon with another layer of aspic and chill again. Repeat once more.

Shred the lettuce or endive and use to line a serving dish and place the salmon on top. Any left-over aspic can be chilled until set hard then chopped up and placed in the dish on top of the lettuce. Serve with mayonnaise (preferably home-made, see page 181). SERVES 10–15

TANGY FISH SALAD

Illustrated on pages 30–1

675 g/1$\frac{1}{2}$ lb smoked haddock fillets, skinned (page 49)
40 g/1$\frac{1}{2}$ oz butter
300 ml/$\frac{1}{2}$ pint natural yogurt
grated rind of 1 lemon
2 sticks celery, chopped
1 red apple, cored and diced
25 g/1 oz walnuts, coarsely chopped
salt and freshly ground pepper
1 lettuce to serve (optional)

DICE the fish into 1-cm/$\frac{1}{2}$-in cubes. Melt the butter in a large saucepan and gently cook the fish for a few minutes on either side. Drain and chill for 2 hours.

Mix the remaining ingredients together and add to the fish. Season to taste. Serve on a bed of lettuce leaves or in individual glasses as a starter. SERVES 6–8

SALMON WITH ORANGE AND MINT SAUCE

4 salmon or salmon trout steaks
about 600 ml / 1 pint court bouillon (page 169)
mint sprigs to garnish

SAUCE
about 30 mint leaves
juice and $\frac{1}{2}$ grated rind of 1 orange
1 teaspoon honey
1 teaspoon redcurrant jelly
3 tablespoons boiling water
2 tablespoons red wine vinegar

SALAD
1 endive or crisp lettuce
$\frac{1}{2}$ cucumber, thinly sliced
$\frac{1}{2}$ bunch watercress
1 bunch spring onions

PLACE the steaks in the warm court bouillon. Bring gently up to simmering, allow to bubble once or twice, then remove from the heat. Turn the steaks over in the poaching liquid, and leave them to cool, covered with a lid or plate. Leave for about 1 hour then lift the steaks out with a slotted spoon and transfer to a plate and leave to chill.

Meanwhile, make the sauce. Very finely chop the mint leaves. Add the orange rind to the mint leaves in a bowl with the honey and redcurrant jelly. Pour over the boiling water and mix well. Then add the juice from the orange and the wine vinegar and leave to chill.

Arrange the endive or lettuce on a serving plate around the salmon steaks, and place the thinly sliced cucumber and watercress sprigs around the edge. Toss a few spring onions, sliced thinly lengthways, over the salad. Spoon a spoonful of sauce over each salmon steak and sprinkle the rest over the salad. Garnish the salmon with sprigs of mint. Drink a good chilled white wine with this lovely fresh salad. SERVES 4

CRAWFISH SALAD

The melon and cucumber make this a particularly refreshing and elegant salad which contrasts pleasingly with the richness of the crawfish.

1 (1.5-kg/3-lb) crawfish
1 clove garlic, crushed
1–2 teaspoons Dijon mustard
½ teaspoon clear honey
4 tablespoons natural yogurt
4 tablespoons mayonnaise (page 181)
salt and freshly ground black pepper
1 endive
½ cucumber, peeled and diced
1 honeydew melon, scooped out and chunked
squeeze of lemon or lime juice
ribbons of lettuce or endive to garnish (optional)
brown bread and butter to serve

COOK the crawfish, if alive, or buy a cooked crawfish from the fishmonger, and extract the meat (see page 50). Reserve the antennae for use as a garnish, if desired. Beat together the garlic, mustard and honey, and gradually add the yogurt to make a smooth mixture. Stir in the mayonnaise to finish the dressing and season to taste with salt and pepper.

On a round platter, make a base of the endive leaves. Make an outer circle of the diced cucumber and chunks of melon. Combine the crawfish meat with the dressing and heap into the centre. Sprinkle with lemon or lime juice and cover with ribbons of endive or lettuce to garnish, if liked. Serve with brown bread and butter. You could also use the reserved spiny antennae of the crawfish to garnish the dish, if desired. SERVES 4

SMOKED FISH BOARD

I first made this salad arrangement with my own home-smoked grey mullet. It was a delicious combination which can be adapted for all smoked fish.

2 hot-smoked mackerel fillets
2 hot-smoked trout fillets
juice of $\frac{1}{2}$ lemon
1 tablespoon dried dill
2 medium carrots, cut into matchsticks
2 sticks celery, cut into matchsticks
1 cucumber, cut lengthways, deseeded, and cut into matchsticks
1 bunch spring onions, sliced lengthways
2 crunchy red apples, or 1 mango, or 2 kiwi fruit, thinly sliced
granary bread to serve

APPLE AND HORSERADISH SAUCE
4 tablespoons apple purée
1 tablespoon grated horseradish

SOURED CREAM COCKTAIL SAUCE
300 ml/$\frac{1}{2}$ pint soured cream
4 tablespoons Cocktail Sauce (page 182)
50 g/2 oz Philadelphia cream cheese

CUT the smoked fish across the fillets into thick strips about 2.5 cm/1 in wide and 10 cm/4 in long.

On a large wooden board or large, shallow platter, arrange the strips of fillets in fan shapes. Squeeze a little lemon juice over the fish and sprinkle with the dill. Arrange the raw vegetables in between the fish in colourful combinations. The thinly sliced fruit can be arranged at random over the whole arrangement. The fruit is pretty but apart from the visual effect, it provides a lovely accompaniment to the smoked fish.

Make the first sauce by combining the apple purée with the grated horseradish (or horseradish sauce) and serve as a dip.

Blend the ingredients for the second sauce together until smooth.

Serve with granary bread. SERVES 6–8

GRAPEFRUIT AND SHELLFISH SALAD

Illustrated on pages 54–5

2 pink grapefruits
1 crisp lettuce, shredded
$\frac{1}{2}$ cucumber, peeled, deseeded and diced
225 g/8 oz crab meat
175 g/6 oz peeled cooked prawns
1 tablespoon natural yogurt
4 tablespoons mayonnaise (page 181)
squeeze of lime juice
salt and freshly ground black pepper
lime twists or slices and a pinch of cayenne to garnish

SLICE the grapefruit in half, crosswise, and scoop out the segments. Reserve the juice and the grapefruit shells. Chop the segments and combine with half the shredded lettuce, the diced cucumber, the flaked crab meat and prawns.

Beat the yogurt into the mayonnaise, and add a teaspoon of the reserved grapefruit juice, and a squeeze of lime juice. Line the hollowed grapefruit halves with the remaining lettuce and heap in the seafood salad. Spoon over the mayonnaise dressing and garnish with twists or slices of lime and a sprinkle of cayenne. SERVES 4

CEVICHE

It is worth trying marinated fish. The citrus juice marinade has a similar effect on the flesh as cooking by heat. However, if you are still feeling wary, you could scald the fish in boiling water as you are preparing it, but you will not get quite the same effect. It is important to use only very fresh fish for this slightly unusual dish.

8 large fresh scallops or 450 g / 1 lb monkfish
juice of 2 limes
juice of 3 or 4 lemons
fresh coriander leaves to garnish

SALAD
4 tomatoes, quartered
1 green pepper, chopped
1 bunch spring onions, sliced lengthways
1 avocado pear, peeled and stoned
bunch of coarsely chopped parsley or chervil

SALAD DRESSING
1 clove garlic, crushed
150 ml / ¼ pint olive oil
pinch each of salt and freshly ground black pepper
6 drops of Tabasco sauce

PREPARE the scallops as shown on page 53, or skin and bone the monkfish (see page 48). Cut each scallop into 2 to 3 thick slices, or slice the monkfish into medallions. Pour over a mixture of the lemon juice and lime juice, cover with cling film and leave to marinate in the refrigerator for 4 to 6 hours.

Make the dressing by putting all the ingredients in a screw-top jar, tighten the lid and shake well to combine.

Prepare the salad, and toss in the dressing – chill for about 30 minutes.

Drain the marinade juices from the fish, and combine the fish and salad. Garnish with fresh coriander leaves. SERVES 4

FRESH COCKLES WITH PASTA SPIRALS

Cockles and whelks are traditionally eaten with brown vinegar and a shake or two of salt and pepper and very tasty they are too! Whelks can be rather tough and rubbery but can add flavour to soups and stews – however, the charming little cockle is quite underrated in my view. Do try this simple recipe. I think you will be surprised at just how delicious these little shellfish can be. This recipe is very simple yet very good!

350 g / 12 oz wholemeal or white pasta spirals
(or shells)
450 g / 1 lb cockles

DRESSING
150 ml / ¼ pint olive oil
dash of white wine vinegar
3 cloves garlic, crushed
1 teaspoon clear honey
1 teaspoon Dijon mustard

MAKE the dressing by putting all the ingredients together in a screw-top jar and shaking well. Cook the pasta according to the instructions on the packet until *al dente*. Drain and, while hot, toss in the cockles and dressing. Serve warm with a crisp green salad. SERVES 4–6

Snacks and Suppers

Fish – the original fast food. Have you ever considered that there cannot be a more natural and fresh food which can be cooked as quickly and simply as fish?

Busy families, and children in particular, who only have time to clock in and grab a bite before zooming off again, could be encouraged to resist the eternal sandwich, the tin of soup, or the greasy fry-up. There is a more exciting and nutritious (and incidentally, more economical) alternative in fish. Try the Fish and Sorrel Omelette (see page 145) or Smoked Mackerel and Cottage Cheese Flan (see page 153) for variations on familiar themes.

Quick fish snacks can range from, for example, a plate of simply grilled fresh sardines to more imaginative made-up dishes using cold, cooked, or left-over fish. And snack time could be the time when you produce those extra fish cakes or croquettes you stored away in the freezer.

I hope this short chapter will fire your imagination and inspire you to think about fish on those occasions when a delicious, quick and nourishing meal is called for.

Smoked Haddock and Leek Flan (page 149) and Fish Pasties (page 153)

FETTUCINE ALLA TROTA

Illustrated on pages 14–15

This is a substantial and quickly made supper dish using smoked trout.

1 medium onion, finely chopped
2 cloves garlic, finely chopped
1 tablespoon olive oil
4 hot-smoked trout, boned and flaked
450 g/1 lb fresh or dried fettucine
pinch each of salt, black pepper and ground mace
300 ml/½ pint whipping cream
1 tablespoon chopped parsley and 1 teaspoon red lumpfish roe to garnish (optional)

SOFTEN the onion and garlic in the oil then add the flaked trout flesh.

Cook the pasta until *al dente* in plenty of boiling water and drain. Add to the trout mixture, season to taste with the salt, pepper and mace then pour on the cream. Toss together over a high heat for 1 minute and serve sprinkled with chopped parsley and red lumpfish roe, if wished. SERVES 4

SIZZLY WHITING WITH TANGY SAUCE

4 whiting fillets
50 g/2 oz butter
1 tablespoon prepared English mustard
3 tablespoons single cream or natural yogurt
2 teaspoons lemon juice
½ teaspoon Worcestershire sauce

FRY the whiting fillets in the butter for about 4 minutes each side, or cook under the grill, then place the fillets on a serving dish.

Mix together the mustard, cream, lemon juice and Worcestershire sauce and pour this into the pan. Heat through, stirring continuously, but do not boil. Pour the sauce over the fish and serve hot. SERVES 4

HERRINGS IN OATMEAL

Illustrated on page 10

This is a traditional dish from Scotland which makes a very tasty supper, though it is also a marvellous meal at anytime.

8 herring fillets
flour for dusting
freshly ground black pepper
2–3 eggs, beaten
100 g/4 oz porridge oats
1 teaspoon mustard powder
oil for shallow frying

DUST the fillets with the flour seasoned with the pepper. Dip in the egg and coat in the oats mixed with the mustard powder. Heat the oil and shallow fry until golden brown, about 5 minutes each side, turning once. Drain well, and serve piping hot. SERVES 4

PAN-FRIED PIZZA

Illustrated on pages 146–7

This scone-based pizza is very easy to make and cook. You could also make four individual pizzas, about 10-cm/4-in. in diameter, and bake these on a lightly greased baking tray in an oven for about 10 minutes. Another good idea would be to use a lightly buttered Yorkshire Pudding tin for the bases. Try serving this dish with a home-made coleslaw for a change.

FOR THE PIZZA
225 g/8 oz wholemeal or white flour, or half of each
pinch of salt
1 teaspoon baking powder
25–50 g/1–2 oz butter
about 150 ml/¼ pint milk

TOPPING
1 medium onion, finely chopped
1 clove garlic, crushed
a little oil for frying
1 (397-g/14-oz) can chopped tomatoes
1 tablespoon chopped fresh or 1 teaspoon dried mixed herbs
225–350 g/8–12 oz hot-smoked mackerel, roughly flaked
100 g/4 oz peeled cooked prawns
175 g/6 oz Gruyère or Cheddar cheese
50 g/2 oz black olives
chopped parsley

SIFT the flour, salt and baking powder together, rub in the butter until the mixture resembles fine breadcrumbs, then add enough milk to form into a firm scone dough. With cool fingers, lightly pat it into a round pizza shape on a floured work surface. It should be able to fit in a deep-sided frying pan. Heat a little oil in the pan and put in the pizza base. Leave to cook gently for about 10 minutes, occasionally slipping a spatula around the edge of the pizza to prevent it sticking.

Meanwhile, soften the onion and garlic in a little hot oil. Add the tomatoes and herbs and continue to cook until the juice is reduced and thick.

Spoon the tomato mixture onto the pizza and scatter the flaked fish and prawns over. Either top the fish with grated cheese and olives or cut the cheese into strips and make a lattice pattern, arranging the olives in the little squares. Put the pizza under a hot grill and continue to cook until the topping is brown and bubbling. SERVES 4–6

FISH AND SORREL OMELETTE

Illustrated on pages 146–7

This provides a very good light lunch dish. Try it with a crunchy red and green pepper salad dressed with oil and vinegar – a good contrast in bite and texture!

6 eggs
4 tablespoons natural yogurt
1 tablespoon chopped parsley
freshly ground black pepper
25 g/1 oz butter
1 small onion or shallot, finely chopped
12 leaves of sorrel, or spinach, finely chopped
175 g/6 oz cooked white fish fillets (e.g. cod, coley, or haddock)
75 g/3 oz cooked smoked fish fillets (e.g. kipper or mackerel)

BEAT the eggs and yogurt together then add the chopped parsley and pepper to taste. Melt the butter in a large omelette pan and cook the onion until pale and soft. Add the chopped sorrel or spinach and stir for about 1 minute, until the leaves soften. Then add the fish, skinned (see page 49) and chopped into chunks. Pour in the beaten egg mixture and cook in the normal way for an omelette. Finish by browning under the grill. SERVES 2

Fish and Sorrel Omelette (above), Cheesey Fish Burgers (page 148) and Pan-fried Pizza (above)

SEAFOOD RISSOTTO

A basic rissotto is a quick, simple and attractive base for almost any kind of seafood. It is especially attractive to children, and useful too for using up left-over cooked fish. You could also serve the rissotto chilled with salad – toss a few seedless white grapes and fresh green herbs into the rissotto and serve on a bed of Chinese leaves with a light mayonnaise dressing.

1 clove garlic, crushed
1 medium onion, finely chopped
1 tablespoon vegetable oil
75 g/3 oz butter
450 g/1 lb basmati or patna rice
600 ml/1 pint fish stock (page 170)
600 ml/1 pint boiling water
175 g/6 oz button mushrooms, finely sliced
225 g/8 oz petit pois
1 (184-g/6½-oz) can pimentos, chopped
salt and freshly ground black pepper
450 g/1 lb firm white fish (cod, hake, eel, etc.)
cooked and flaked, or cut into bite-sized pieces
225 g/8 oz peeled cooked prawns
225 g/8 oz canned or fresh mussels
4 tablespoons chopped parsley

In a large, heavy frying or sauté pan, soften the crushed garlic and chopped onion in the oil and 25 g/1 oz butter until pale and transparent, then stir in the rice until it is glistening and hot. Pour in the stock and boiling water, bring up to just simmering and give a gentle stir or two, cover and leave to cook.

Meanwhile, melt the remaining butter in another pan and gently cook the mushrooms – remove with a slotted spoon and reserve.

When the rice is almost cooked, add the petit pois and chopped pimento and season the rice to taste with a pinch of salt and freshly ground pepper. At this stage you may need to add a little more liquid – use more stock, or white wine or boiling water. Cook for a further 2 or 3 minutes, then tip in the seafood and mushrooms and carefully turn the rissotto until all is well incorporated and hot – be careful not to overcook at this stage. Scatter the chopped parsley over the rissotto and take the pan straight to the table to serve. A tossed green salad is good with this rissotto. SERVES 6–8

CHEESEY FISH BURGERS

———— *Illustrated on pages 146–7* ————

350 g/12 oz cooked, flaked white fish (coley, whiting or pollack)
450 g/1 lb mashed potato
2 tablespoons chopped parsley
salt and freshly ground black pepper
225 g/8 oz Cheddar cheese, grated
2 eggs, beaten
porridge oats or sesame seeds to coat

Fork the flaked fish into the mashed potato. Add the chopped parsley and seasoning to taste. Scoop out a large spoonful, and mould into a ball shape in your hand (flour your hands first if the mixture is sticky.) Press a few small spoonfuls of grated Cheddar into the middle of each ball. Flatten into a burger shape and continue until all the mixture has been used. Dip the burgers in the beaten egg and coat in porridge oats, or sesame seeds. Chill for 30 minutes then bake, grill, or shallow fry and serve with grilled tomato halves and green vegetables or salad. SERVES 4

PAN-FRIED BUBBLY

This dish has proved very popular with children. You can use other small whole fish instead of sardines. It makes a very colourful and attractive dish.

675 g / 1½ lb potatoes, cooked and mashed
salt and freshly ground black pepper
1 egg, beaten
1 small onion, grated
3 tablespoons oil
1 large green pepper
1 (227-g/8-oz) can tomatoes
1 tablespoon concentrated tomato purée
½ teaspoon dried mixed herbs
8 fresh sardines, cleaned
50 g / 2 oz Cheddar cheese, grated
1 tablespoon chopped parsley to garnish

MIX the mashed potato, seasoning, egg and onion together. Heat the oil in a large frying pan, add the potato mixture and smooth with a knife or spatula. Gently fry in the oil for 20 to 25 minutes until golden brown underneath.

Meanwhile, scorch the skin of the pepper under a hot grill and peel, then cut lengthways into strips. Mix the tomatoes, tomato purée and herbs together and heat gently.

Pour the tomato mixture over the potatoes in the frying pan. On top of this form a wheel shape with the sardines, with their heads pointing outwards – and arrange strips of pepper between each sardine. Grill under a moderate heat for 5 minutes or until the sardines are nearly cooked, then sprinkle over the grated cheese, turn up the heat and grill until the top is golden and bubbling. Garnish with the parsley and cut the bubbly into wedges. Serve, if liked, with a green vegetable. SERVES 4

SMOKED HADDOCK AND LEEK FLAN

Illustrated on page 142

This is a very quick flan to make. In a flash you have a lovely lunch or snack which can be served with a crisp green salad and crunchy bread, or jacket potatoes.

1 quantity Shortcrust Pastry (page 62)
600 ml / 1 pint milk
50 g / 2 oz flour
50 g / 2 oz butter
salt and freshly ground black pepper
350 g / 12 oz smoked haddock, flaked
450 g / 1 lb leeks, finely chopped
finely chopped green part of the leeks to garnish

USE the pastry to line a 25-cm/10-in flan tin or dish and bake blind in a moderately hot oven (200 c, 400 F, gas 6) for 10 minutes.

Put the milk, flour and butter together in a saucepan and bring gently up to simmering, whisking with a balloon whisk or stirring with a wooden spoon continuously as it thickens. Continue to simmer for 1 to 2 minutes, until smooth and creamy, then season with salt and pepper. Take off the heat, and fold in the flaked smoked haddock and finely chopped raw leeks. Pour into the flan case and bake in a moderately hot oven (200 c, 400 F, gas 6) for 20 minutes. Serve immediately, garnished with the finely chopped green part of the leeks. SERVES 4–6

NOTE: You can enrich the sauce when you take it off the heat by adding 50 g / 2 oz butter or a beaten egg yolk.

JACKET POTATOES

The renewed popularity of potatoes after years of being wrongly labelled as fattening is very welcome. There are many varieties of potato to choose from and potatoes and fish are wonderful partners, providing nutritious and balanced meals for everyone – as simply or as fussily as you like. You can cook jacket potatoes very quickly in the microwave, which makes them an ideal snack or supper – especially for children – or a quick main meal served with green vegetables or salad. Each filling is for four large potatoes. Bake the potatoes in a moderately hot oven (200 c, 400 f, gas 6) for about 1 hour or at full power in the microwave for about 20 minutes.

COTTAGE CHEESE, COD AND KIPPER FILLING

———— *Illustrated opposite* ————

2 tablespoons sunflower seeds
a little oil
100 g/4 oz cod, cooked and flaked
100 g/4 oz kipper fillet, cooked, skinned and cut into thin strips
225 g/8 oz cottage cheese
2 tablespoons chopped parsley to garnish

Sauté the sunflower seeds in a little oil. Mix together the cod, kipper fillets and cottage cheese and use to stuff the potatoes. Garnish with the sunflower seeds and parsley.

SHRIMP AND SPRING ONION FILLING

———— *Illustrated opposite* ————

225 g/8 oz peeled cooked shrimps
150 ml/$\frac{1}{4}$ pint soured cream
150 ml/$\frac{1}{4}$ pint natural yogurt
a few drops of Tabasco sauce
4 spring onions, finely chopped
pinch of freshly ground black pepper

When the potatoes are ready, cut almost in half lengthways and crossways to form a criss-cross. Combine the filling ingredients and heap into the potatoes. Garnish with a few chopped green bits of spring onions.

SALMON AND SOURED CREAM FILLING

———— *Illustrated opposite* ————

225 g/8 oz cold poached salmon (or drained tin)
300 ml/$\frac{1}{2}$ pint soured cream
1 teaspoon fresh lemon juice
2 teaspoons chopped fresh or $\frac{1}{2}$ teaspoon dried thyme
pinch each of salt and freshly ground black pepper
50 g/2 oz flaked almonds, toasted, to garnish

Flake the cooked salmon, removing any skin and bones. Mix together the filling ingredients, place in the middle of the baked potatoes and garnish with the almonds.

Jacket Potatoes with Salmon and Soured Cream Filling (above), Shrimp and Spring Onion Filling (above) and Cottage Cheese, Cod and Kipper Filling (above)

BRIE AND COD FILLING

50 g/2 oz butter, softened
1 egg
100 g/4 oz Brie or grated Gruyère
225 g/8 oz cooked flaked cod
salt and pepper
cayenne
1–2 tablespoons chopped parsley, to garnish

CUT the potatoes in half lengthways, scoop out the cooked potato and mash well with the butter, egg and de-rinded Brie or grated Gruyère. Fork in the flaked fish, season to taste with salt and pepper then heap back into the potato skins. Dot with a little butter and a dusting of cayenne and bake in a hot oven (220 C, 425 F, gas 7) for 10 minutes, until golden. Scatter with the parsley before serving.

CRAB CAKES

450 g/1 lb crab meat
50 g/2 oz fresh breadcrumbs
1 egg, beaten
5 tablespoons mayonnaise
1 tablespoon Worcestershire sauce
1 teaspoon prepared mustard
pinch each of salt and black pepper
oil for frying
lemon wedges to serve

PREPARE the crab as explained on page 52 or buy a prepared crab from the fishmonger, then mix together the brown and white meat; try not to break up the flakes of white meat too much. Combine the remaining ingredients, and fold in the crab meat. Heat the oil in a shallow pan, and using a spoon (I use an ice-cream or potato scoop) drop the mixture into the hot oil and fry on each side for 2 minutes, or until golden brown. Remove with a perforated spoon and drain on absorbent kitchen paper. Serve immediately with wedges of lemon. SERVES 4

FISH CROQUETTES

I love the crunchy texture of the sesame coating of these croquettes, but you could substitute toasted breadcrumbs if you prefer. They are swiftly prepared using a food processor, and ideal for freezing for up to six months. They can be baked or microwaved direct from the freezer.

450 g/1 lb cooked white fish fillets (cod, hake, coley or brill)
450 g/1 lb cooked potato, diced
1 bulb fennel, finely chopped
2 tablespoons roughly chopped parsley
1 large or 2 small eggs
25 g/1 oz soft margarine
pinch each of salt and freshly ground black pepper
100 g/4 oz sesame seeds
a little vegetable oil (optional)

REMOVE the skin from the fish fillets and flake the fish, making sure there are no bones. Place in a food processor or blender with the diced potato, chopped fennel, parsley, egg and margarine. Blend until all the ingredients are well mashed and begin to leave the side of the bowl. Transfer to a mixing bowl, season to taste and place in a refrigerator. Chill for about an hour until nice and firm to handle. Shape the mixture into croquettes and, on a large plate, roll each croquette carefully in sesame seeds until well coated.

The croquettes can now be gently fried in a little vegetable oil (turn them carefully with tongs as they brown) or placed on a lightly greased baking tray and baked in a hot oven (220 C, 425 F, gas 7) for about 12 minutes, turning once during the cooking time.

Serve immediately – three or four for each person – with a helping of steamed strips of carrot, parsley and spring onion, and perhaps a spoonful or two of tomato sauce (see page 176). SERVES 4

FISH PASTIES

Illustrated on page 142

An excellent package or convenience meal for picnics, *al fresco* suppers, or packed lunches. Or – dare I suggest it – a TV meal. Once the preparation is done, and the pasties are cooking or cooked, there is no washing up or cleaning away to do. Wrap the pasties in thick paper serviettes for family and friends to eat in their hands.

1 quantity Shortcrust Pastry (page 62)
450 g / 1 lb potatoes, peeled and finely sliced
1 medium onion or 2 leeks, finely sliced
1 tablespoon freshly chopped parsley
pinch each of salt and freshly ground black pepper
1 tablespoon single cream
350 g / 12 oz white fish fillets, skinned and cut into bite-sized pieces (page 49)
100 g / 4 oz hot-smoked fish fillet or smoked salmon scraps, cut into bite-sized pieces
1 egg, beaten, for glazing

THE pastry should be chilled for at least 30 minutes before using – some pastry experts recommend that pastry is made the day before and kept in the refrigerator for best results.

As all the vegetable ingredients for the filling are not pre-cooked it is important that they are sliced very thinly.

Roll out the pastry on a board floured with wholemeal flour (this gives a lovely speckled texture to the finished pasty). With a large side plate or small dinner plate, cut out four rounds.

In a large bowl, using your fingers, toss together the prepared vegetables, herbs and seasoning and moisten with the cream. Heap 2 to 3 tablespoons of this vegetable mixture in the centre of each pasty. Top each with the white and smoked fish.

Bring up each side of the pasty to the centre, and crimp. The filling should be generous, and teased into the pastry. If you have too little mixture the filling will shrink during cooking and your pasty will be half hollow. Any holes in the pastry from stretching can be patched with left-over scraps. Using a fish slice, carefully transfer to a lightly greased baking tray and push over the crimped edge to form a crescent shape. Brush the pasties with the beaten egg and bake in a hot oven (220 c, 425 f, gas 7) for 10 to 15 minutes for the pastry to set and brown. Then turn down the heat to moderate (180 c, 350 f, gas 4) and continue to bake for about 30 minutes, until the contents have cooked deliciously in their own juices. Test that the filling is cooked with a skewer. Serve immediately or wrap in aluminium foil and put in an insulated picnic bag for a picnic outing or barbecue. SERVES 4

SMOKED MACKEREL AND COTTAGE CHEESE FLAN

A very simple and quick recipe. Substitute smoked salmon, trout, or kipper fillets for the smoked mackerel if you wish. Serve it hot or cold with a crisp green salad.

1 quantity Shortcrust Pastry (page 62)
225 g / 8 oz hot-smoked mackerel fillets
2 eggs
225 g / 8 oz cottage cheese
2 tomatoes, chopped
salt and freshly ground black pepper

USE the pastry to line a 20-cm / 8-in flan tin or dish and bake blind in a moderately hot oven (200 c, 400 f, gas 6) for 10 to 12 minutes. Remove the skin from the smoked mackerel fillets and flake or slice the flesh into small pieces. In a mixing bowl, beat the eggs and combine with the cottage cheese, fish and chopped tomatoes. Season to taste with salt and freshly ground pepper.

Put this mixture into your pre-baked flan case and bake in a moderate oven (180 c, 350 f, gas 4) for about 25 minutes. SERVES 4

Barbecues, Breakfasts and Brunches

We cannot count on getting good weather for our British summer, yet we will endure the most miserable summer's day for the delights of a barbecue sizzling with a feast of fish. For all sorts of occasions – summer lunches, children's parties, picnics and even bonfire nights – fish and shellfish are the ideal foods to barbecue. It is often on holiday that we have the time and opportunity to try all sorts of different fresh fish in a relaxed *al fresco* style, and it is often the memory of sunny days by the sea with wonderful brunches or barbecues of seafood that inspire the enterprising cook to be more adventurous in the family kitchen.

You may think that cooked breakfasts are a thing of the past, but the recipes in this chapter will rapidly change your mind. Who can resist the temptation of the classic Kedgeree (see page 160) and children, in particular, will find it fun to try cooking kippers by the means suggested in Jugged Kippers with Scrambled Egg (see page 161). What could be a better start to the day than fuelling up on fish at breakfast!

Brunches can provide a quick and easy meal when you opt for Bubble and Squeak with Fish (see page 164) or try the Coastguards' Herring Flippits (see page 161). These are ideal for people who do not have the time or chance to sit down to a proper meal or for those families who are eating at different times of the day.

Sprats Boursin (page 156) and Smoked Trout Fishcakes (page 157)

BARBECUED SPRATS

Sprats are an oily fish – a member of the herring family – and ideal for the barbecue, or for grilling indoors.

675 g/1½ lb sprats
1 teaspoon prepared English mustard mixed with 2 tablespoons natural yogurt
Cold Tomato Sauce (page 177)
Tartare Sauce (page 182)

ASK your fishmonger to clean the sprats, or do this yourself (see page 44). Allow the burning charcoal to get really hot and turn grey, then place the sprats on an oiled rack over the barbecue and grill for 2 to 3 minutes each side until crisp. Spear them with a fork and dip into one of the above sauces – the yogurt mixed with English mustard is particularly good. SERVES 4–6

SPRATS BOURSIN

Illustrated on page 154

salt and freshly ground black pepper
450 g/1 lb sprats, cleaned and boned (page 45)
1 (142-g/5-oz) packet Boursin cream cheese, softened
flour for dusting

SEASON the sprats, spread the insides with the cheese and fold over to reshape the sprat. Dust lightly in flour then place on the oiled rack of the barbecue, turning once. Cook for a few minutes on each side. You can remove the heads from the sprats before cooking, if wished. SERVES 4

TROUT COOKED IN NEWSPAPER

This unusual but highly effective method comes from a Victorian angling book and works equally well with a conventional oven, barbecue or bonfire!

4 trout, cleaned
salt and freshly ground pepper
3 sheets newspaper

SEASON the trout inside and wrap in the sheets of newspaper, tucking the ends in neatly. Soak the parcel in cold water and cook for 25 to 30 minutes or until the paper is dry. When you cut open the paper the skin will peel off, leaving a moist and succulent fish. If the fish is to be served cold, leave to cool in the paper. Large salmon trout can be cooked in the same way using 8 or 9 layers of paper for a 1.5 kg/3 lb fish and cooking for 1 hour. SERVES 4

BARBECUED SCALLOPS

12 scallops
24 rashers streaky bacon
lemon wedges
bay leaves

OPEN and prepare the scallops (see page 53), then cut in half. Wrap each piece of scallop in a rasher of bacon and thread onto a skewer, alternating with wedges of lemon and bay leaves. Cook on the barbecue for about 3 minutes, until the bacon is crisp and brown. SERVES 3–4

COD KEBABS WITH BARBECUE SAUCE

Illustrated on page 10

675 g / 1½ lb cod steaks
12 large bay leaves
12–16 button mushrooms, stalks removed

SAUCE/MARINADE
2 teaspoons prepared mustard
4 teaspoons Worcestershire sauce
4 tablespoons wine vinegar
4 tablespoons olive or sunflower oil
4 tablespoons tomato ketchup

REMOVE the skin and bones from the cod and cut into chunks. Place in a glass or earthenware bowl. Combine the marinade/sauce ingredients, pour over the cod and leave for 20 minutes turning occasionally.

Make sure the barbecue is good and hot. Oil the kebab skewers and thread on the chunks of cod interspersed with the bay leaves and mushrooms. Grill over the barbecue, turning and basting with the marinade. Serve immediately with a crisp green salad, and pour the remaining marinade/sauce over the kebabs on the individual plates. SERVES 4

SMOKED TROUT FISHCAKES

Illustrated on page 154

1 small onion, finely chopped
1–2 tablespoons oil
225 g / 8 oz smoked trout flesh, flaked
450 g / 1 lb cold mashed potato
2–3 tablespoons chopped herbs (parsley, chives or fennel)
salt and freshly ground black pepper
seasoned flour
1 egg, beaten
dried breadcrumbs

SOFTEN the onion in the oil then add to the smoked trout, potato, herbs and seasoning to taste. Mix together well then mould into fishcakes with a spoon or using your hands. Coat well with the seasoned flour then cover with egg and breadcrumbs. Bake in a hot oven (220c, 425f, gas 7) for 10 to 15 minutes, turning once. (Alternatively, shallow fry in a little oil until crisp and golden on both sides.) SERVES 4

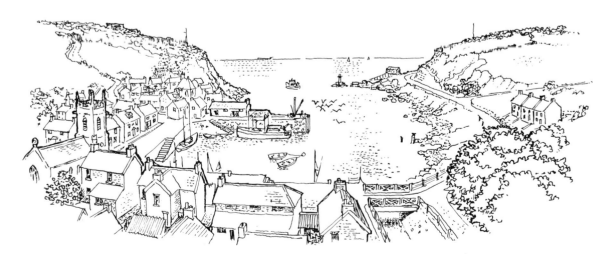

BARBECUED HAKE WITH COURGETTE PARCELS

A lovely combination of taste and texture.

4 hake cutlets, about 2.5 cm/1 in thick
4 medium-large courgettes
salt and freshly ground black pepper
100 g/4 oz blanched almonds, slivered
25 g/1 oz butter

MARINADE
4 tablespoons olive oil
2 tablespoons orange juice
2 tablespoons lemon juice
pinch of salt
5 peppercorns, bruised
1 very finely chopped shallot
1 tablespoon finely chopped fennel

FIRST combine the marinade ingredients. Wash and pat dry the hake cutlets. Pour the marinade over the hake and marinate for 1 to 1½ hours, turning occasionally. Meanwhile, lightly butter four aluminium foil parcel shapes. Thinly slice the courgettes, and put a serving onto each parcel. Season lightly, sprinkle over a few almonds and add a tiny dot of butter. Seal the parcels and place over the heat. As soon as you hear the courgettes hissing or sizzling, put the hake steaks on the oiled grid of the barbecue and, basting frequently with the marinade, cook for a few minutes on each side.

Put the foil parcels on individual plates, peel back to reveal the courgettes in their own juices (it does not matter if they are still slightly crunchy), and place a hake cutlet alongside. Sprinkle with a little chopped fennel and serve with a plain potato salad. Incidentally, you could use a tablespoon of the marinade to dress the potatoes while hot. Otherwise a good vinaigrette can be used.
SERVES 4

BARBECUED DUBLIN BAY PRAWNS

These large prawns are in fact correctly called Norway lobsters, though they are also referred to as scampi or langoustines in the fishmongers'.

12–16 Dublin Bay prawns
1 large green pepper
2 lemons
a little oil

TO BASTE
3–4 tablespoons olive oil
2 tablespoons lemon juice
salt and freshly ground black pepper

WASH the prawns under cold running water and dry on absorbent kitchen paper. Cut the green pepper into large chunks, removing the seeds and pith first. Cut the lemons into wedges. Use the oil to grease lightly four skewers and thread the prawns on to them, alternating with the pepper and lemon wedges. Combine the olive oil, lemon juice and seasoning to taste and use to baste the prawns as they grill over the barbecue for 10 to 15 minutes. SERVES 4

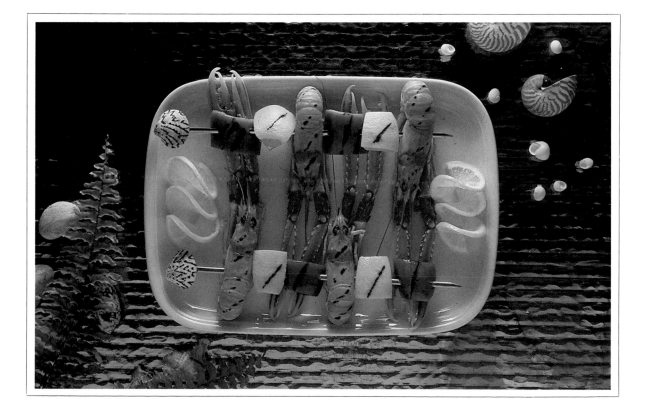

KEDGEREE

Illustrated on pages 162–3

Lovely for breakfast – or supper. This dish is good with chutney or tomato relish.

450 g/1 lb smoked haddock fillets
milk for poaching
1 small onion or 2–3 spring onions, finely chopped
50 g/2 oz butter
225 g/8 oz cooked long-grain rice
4 hard-boiled eggs, chopped

POACH the haddock in the milk (see page 25), lift off the skin and flake the flesh. Cook the onion or spring onions in the butter, add the rice and stir as it gently heats up. Add the flaked haddock, taking care not to break up the flesh too much, and add the hard-boiled eggs. SERVES 4

HERRING ROES ON MUFFINS

Illustrated on pages 162–3

This makes a very tasty and unusual breakfast. Melt 25 g/1 oz butter in a sauté pan, and add a little prepared English mustard. Gently fry the roes for 4 minutes on each side and serve them on thinly buttered, toasted wholemeal muffins or crumpets. SERVES 4

JUGGED KIPPERS WITH SCRAMBLED EGG

Illustrated on pages 162–3

COOK the kippers as described on page 33 and serve with a portion of scrambled eggs garnished with chopped parsley, lemon wedges and wholemeal toast. SERVES 4

FINNAN HADDOCK ON TOAST

FLAKE 225 g/8 oz of cooked Finnan haddock and mix with softened margarine, butter or a little cream. Spread straight on to hot wholemeal toast and brown under the grill. These should be served with poached eggs. SERVES 2–3

CODDLED EGG AND HADDOCK

This is a favourite breakfast of mine, and is ideal for microwave ovens.

15 g/½ oz butter
225–350 g/8–12 oz smoked haddock, cut into strips
50 g/2 oz button mushrooms (optional)
4 teaspoons milk
freshly ground black pepper
4 eggs
Worcestershire sauce and wholemeal toast to serve

LIGHTLY butter four ramekin or soufflé dishes. Fill the bottom of each with strips of smoked haddock. Cover with very thinly sliced mushrooms, if you wish, and put in about 1 teaspoon milk (or cream for special breakfasts) and a little pepper. Break an egg on top of the fish and bake in a hot oven (220 c, 425 f, gas 7) for 10 minutes. If cooking in a microwave, remember to pierce the egg yolk with a knife or cocktail stick before cooking on full power for about 3 minutes.

Serve with Worcestershire sauce to taste and wholemeal toast. SERVES 4

FISHY SCRAMBLED EGGS

SCRAMBLE 4 eggs and add chopped parsley and cooked, flaked kipper. Serve on toast. SERVES 4

COASTGUARDS' HERRING FLIPPITS

100 g/4 oz self-raising flour
pinch each of salt and black pepper
1 egg
a little cold water
2 herrings or 4 herring fillets
25 g/1 oz butter
1–2 tablespoons oil
1–2 tablespoons prepared mustard
lemon wedges to serve

SIFT together the flour and salt. Add the egg and sufficient cold water to make a thick dropping consistency, beating continuously with a balloon whisk.

Meanwhile, divide the herrings into four fillets (see page 47) if you have not bought fillets. Cook the fillets under the grill, with dots of butter. Heat a little oil in a frying pan and drop spoonfuls of the batter mixture in to form the flippits (like small pancakes). Cook for 2 minutes then 'flip' them over; continue to cook as they bubble up and rise slightly. Turn the herring fillets under the grill and continue cooking for 4 minutes. Flippits must be served hot straight away – they are not so good if they are kept warm. Spread a little mustard on each flippit and top with a herring fillet. Sprinkle over freshly ground black pepper and serve with wedges of lemon. SERVES 4

FISH, MUSHROOM AND MUSTARD QUICHE

1 quantity Shortcrust Pastry (page 62)
2 tablespoons Dijon mustard
225 g/8 oz white fish fillets (e.g. coley, whiting, pollock or cod), cooked, skinned and flaked
100 g/4 oz smoked salmon scraps
75 g/3 oz button mushrooms, finely chopped
100 g/4 oz cottage cheese
150 ml/$\frac{1}{4}$ pint single cream
4 eggs
pinch each of salt and freshly ground black pepper
175 g/6 oz Cheddar cheese, grated
paprika

LINE a 25-cm/10-in flan dish with the pastry and bake blind for 10 minutes. Spread the Dijon mustard over the cooled base of the flan, then arrange the flaked fish and smoked salmon over this. Scatter over the mushrooms. Combine the cottage cheese, cream, eggs, salt and pepper and pour this mixture on top of the fish. Scatter with grated Cheddar and pepper and pour this mixture on top of the fish. Scatter with grated Cheddar and a dusting of paprika. Bake in a hot oven (220 c, 425 f, gas 7) for 10 minutes, then reduce the temperature to moderately hot (220 c, 400 f, gas 6) for a further 15 minutes. SERVES 4–6

Kedgeree (page 160), Herring Roes on Muffins (page 160) and Jugged Kippers with Scrambled Egg (page 160)

BUBBLE AND SQUEAK WITH FISH

Also known as colcannon, this Irish recipe is usually served with bacon or sausages, but is even more delicious with fish. Bubble and squeak is a versatile way of using up left-overs with the base of mashed potato and cooked cabbage, and can be a cunning way of tempting faddy children into enjoying a tasty and nutritious meal.

1 medium onion, finely chopped
25 g / 1 oz butter or margarine
450 g / 1 lb mashed potato
225 g / 8 oz very lightly cooked cabbage, chopped
225 g / 8 oz cooked white fish fillets, skinned and flaked
1 tablespoon finely chopped parsley
pinch of freshly grated nutmeg
pinch each of salt and freshly ground black pepper
1–2 tablespoons vegetable oil

FIRST of all, soften the chopped onion over a gentle heat in the butter or margarine until pale but not browned. Lift out with a perforated spoon and drain well on absorbent kitchen paper. In a large bowl, mix together the mashed potato, onion, cabbage, flaked fish, parsley and seasonings.

In a heavy frying pan or skillet, heat up enough oil to cover the base of the pan – pour off any excess. Make sure the pan and oil are really hot before putting in the bubble and squeak mixture and forking it down in a large pancake shape, to cover the base of the pan completely. Turn down the heat to let the bubble and squeak cook gently for about 10 minutes, or until the underside of it has formed a crispy brown base. To turn the bubble and squeak, it is a good idea to cut it in half and turn each half separately. You can push the two halves together as it continues to cook for a further 10 minutes, or until the bottom has also formed a crisp brown crust.

Remove the pan from the heat, and cut the bubble and squeak into four wedges. Children might like this with tomato ketchup – but tartare or horseradish sauce are also good accompaniments. SERVES 4

KIPPER CAKES

350 g / 12 oz kipper fillets, skinned
50 g / 2 oz butter, softened
2 eggs, beaten
pinch each of black pepper and cayenne
100 g / 4 oz dried breadcrumbs
a little oil (optional)
apple purée to serve

POUND the kipper fillets and bind together with the butter and half the beaten egg. Season with pepper and cayenne to taste.

Shape into small rissole shapes and chill for at least 10 minutes, then dip in the remaining beaten egg and coat in breadcrumbs. Either fry gently in a little oil or brown in the oven or under the grill. Serve with a tart apple purée. SERVES 3–4

SPICY PITTA PARCELS

——— Illustrated on pages 14–15 ———

450 g/1 lb ling, pollack or firm white fish fillets
2 pitta breads
squeeze of lemon juice
dash of Tabasco sauce (optional)

MARINADE
4 tablespoons oil
2 tablespoons wine vinegar
1 teaspoon Worcestershire sauce
½ teaspoon chilli sauce
salt and freshly ground black pepper

SALAD
1 small onion, sliced
50 g/2 oz cabbage, finely shredded
1 stick celery, sliced
½ green pepper, deseeded and cut into small strips
1–2 tablespoons vinaigrette dressing (page 184)

CUT the fish into medium-sized strips and place in a bowl. Mix the marinade ingredients together and pour over the fish. Allow to marinate for at least 1 hour. Toss the salad vegetables together in a bowl and moisten with the vinaigrette dressing. Season to taste.

Cut each of the pitta breads in half lengthways. Using a sharp knife, and keeping the halves whole, split open. Half-fill each one with salad.

Drain the fish and reserve the marinade. Place the fish under a hot grill for 10 minutes, brushing occasionally with the marinade. Spoon the cooked fish into the half-filled pitta breads and season with a little lemon juice and Tabasco sauce, if using. SERVES 4

PAUPIETTES DE SOLE MORNAY

I include this recipe from *When Cook is Away* by Catherine Ives, published in 1928 – little could she have known then that her recipe would be ideal for re-heating in microwave cookers!

25 g/1 oz butter
4 sole fillets
salt and pepper
1 teaspoon lemon juice
300 ml/½ pint fish stock (page 170)
4 potatoes, baked in their jackets
450 ml/¾ pint Mornay Sauce (page 173)
15–25 g/½–1 oz Parmesan cheese, grated

BUTTER an ovenproof dish. Sprinkle the sole fillets with salt, pepper and lemon juice. Roll them up and put them in the dish. Pour in the stock, cover the dish with buttered grease-proof paper and bake in a moderately hot oven (200 c, 400 F, gas 6) for 10 minutes.

Cut a slice off each potato lengthways. Scoop out the insides of the potatoes. Mash these in a bowl with a fork and mix in the Mornay Sauce. Replace some of this purée in the potatoes, put a fillet of sole in each, cover them with the remaining purée, sprinkle a little Parmesan on top and add one or two tiny knobs of butter. Put the filled potatoes on a baking tray and cook in a hot oven (220 c, 425 F, gas 7) or under a grill for about 10 minutes until brown. SERVES 4

Sauces and Dressings

It is a pity that there has always been a certain mystique surrounding the making of sauces because, although it is true that a few of the great classic sauces do take a little time, patience and practice to perfect, many excellent sauces can be conjured up in a matter of minutes. You can also take short cuts with food processors or liquidisers. To add body and flavour to the simplest of sauces or dressings, remember to add a little of the delicious cooking juices from whatever fish you are cooking.

You may sometimes prefer to enjoy your fresh fish on its own but if you do decide to make a sauce bear in mind that its purpose is not to *disguise* but to enhance and highlight the flavour of the fish you are cooking. A good sauce can really make a simple dish special. Piquant sauces help to offset the richness of some fish, like mackerel or herring, and the acidity of lemon or other citrus fruits can heighten the flavour of many varieties of white fish. Sometimes a sensitive flourish is called for and the cunning use of a savoury butter or dressing can transform the simplest fish dish into a really special offering.

Cod Cutlets with Parsley Sauce (page 173) and
Plaice Rolls with Mushroom Sauce (page 173)

SAUCES, STOCKS, DRESSINGS AND MARINADES

WITH a few exceptions, the flavour of really fresh fish speaks for itself, and should not be drowned in heavy, rich sauces. Certainly on no account should a heavy, thick sauce be used to disguise fish!

Rather, good and imaginative sauces and dressings should highlight and enhance the taste of fish, make a delicate and contrasting accompaniment, and compliment the character of the fish being served.

Fish can be served with the most simple of sauces and dressings – the reduced cooking juices and liquid from the pan with a handful of fresh herbs, a tiny knob of butter to enrichen (if desired) and appropriate seasonings. They can be based on the classic sauces of fish cookery; or they can be fruit or vegetable purées, blended with yogurt, crème fraîche, fromage blanc, or any of the growing range of low-fat dairy products now appearing on the market.

A NOTE ON INGREDIENTS

I love the modern trend towards healthy cooking. Its lightness and freshness is a joy, and especially complimentary for fish, which is so low in fat and so easily digested. You will undo all the good you have done by grilling, baking or poaching your fish with the minimum of fat and fuss if you always smother it with a very rich and floury sauce.

However, many of the more traditional sauces remain firm favourites, and I include the basic recipes for these in this chapter. But it is sensible for us to move slightly away from the British tradition of using rich ingredients in our cooking, as research into nutrition and health indicates that we should cut down on all fats and reduce our overall intake of fats in our daily diet.

I am sure that the occasional tablespoon or two of double cream does no harm, but wherever possible try to substitute yogurt, or simply thin down cream or mayonnaise with yogurt for a lighter and healthier result.

The butter-versus-polyunsaturated margarine controversy continues. In general it may be a good idea to cut down on butter but, just sometimes, nothing else will quite do! If oil is called for in a sauce or dressing, choose a good olive oil, or polyunsaturated oils such as corn, sesame, sunflower, or safflower oil. Sauces need only a pinch of salt, but you could try using a little more herbs, spices or lemon juice instead of salt to give extra flavour, if required.

NOTES ON COOKING SAUCES

The consistency of sauces should vary according to the part they play in the recipe. A sauce served separately needs to be 'flowing', whereas a sauce that is an integral part of the dish needs to be slightly thicker and of 'coating' consistency. It is very fashionable and smart to serve food on top of sauces, and this is particularly attractive for starters. Even thicker sauces serve to bind or hold together 'made-up' fish dishes, such as rissoles.

Sauces based on purées of fruit or vegetables, and combined with low-fat cheese or yogurt, or stock, can be served separately. As many of them are such a pretty colour, try pouring or spooning them onto the plate with the fish arranged on top or at the side to make a delightful and contrasting colourful presentation.

I think it is well worth the little extra effort

needed to make home-made stocks, as these will transform a mediocre sauce into an excellent one! If you really do not have the time or the ingredients to hand for making a good fish stock for a sauce, you could use white wine and a dissolved vegetable stock cube; but personally I do dislike the salty and 'manufactured' taste of them.

Herbs and spices should be used with a certain amount of discretion so that their distinctive flavours enhance rather than dominate the fish. There is no limit to the uses and combinations of herbs and spices so do experiment with your sauce-making and remember that fresh herbs, and freshly ground spices, will produce better results than dried herbs or powdered spices. Make sure that dried herbs and spices have not been at the back of your cupboard for years as the little flavour left in them will be dry and musty tasting.

Sometimes, left-over wine, or very cheap wine, is fine to use in sauces. But if you are cooking a really superior fish, it is wise to use a good quality wine. Again, experimentation is recommended – a lady wrote to me once to say that by accident she had poured her whisky and ginger ale into a sauce for scallops! She pressed on regardless and assures me that the result was excellent though I have yet to try it!

The following pages will give you the basics of stock making, sauces and dressings, and variations of these sauces can also be found here.

COURT BOUILLON

Court bouillon is the term used for a flavoured stock which can be made into a sauce, soup or stew, or in which fish or shellfish can be cooked.

1.15 litres/2 pints water
225 g/8 oz carrots, chopped
2 medium onions, sliced
1 stick celery, chopped
1 bouquet garni (parsley, bay leaf and thyme)
6 black peppercorns, bruised
300 ml/½ pint white wine

PUT everything into a large saucepan and bring to the boil. Simmer for 1 hour, strain and leave to cool. MAKES 1.4 LITRES/2½ PINTS

COURT BOUILLON FOR FRESHWATER FISH

USE the same ingredients as above, but add 250 ml/8 fl oz white wine vinegar, or tarragon vinegar. This is the stock to use for salmon and trout. MAKES 1.75 LITRES/3 PINTS

GOOD FISH STOCK

Ask your fishmonger for bones from fish like turbot or Dover sole, if possible, to use in a stock; or use a whole cheap fish like whiting for a really good stock. Do not use oily fish for stock.

675 g/1½ lb bones and trimmings from white fish
900 ml/1½ pints water
1 onion, sliced
1 carrot, chopped
1 leek, chopped
300 ml/½ pint white wine or cider
6 peppercorns, bruised
1 bouquet garni (optional)

PUT everything except the peppercorns into a large saucepan, bring to the boil, and simmer for 30 minutes, skimming off the scum from time to time. Add the peppercorns for the last 10 minutes of cooking time. MAKES 1.15 LITRES/2 PINTS

MILK, LEMON AND HERB STOCK

This is good for poaching fish and needs no preliminary cooking – it can be used when the fish is removed to make a sauce or flavour a dressing.

300 ml/½ pint milk
300 ml/½ pint water
2–3 lemons, peeled and sliced
1 bouquet garni

POACH the fish in this mixture but do not allow it to boil. Transfer the fish to a heated serving dish and use the stock as required. MAKES 600 ML/1 PINT

USE OF STOCKS

Now you have four basic, simple stocks to play around with. You can add herbs or other seasonings according to the character of the dish you are cooking, bearing in mind the following points.

1. The court bouillon can be used for cooking fish, then reduced by boiling down hard to one third of the original quantity. This concentrates the flavour and thickens the stock. You can then continue to use this reduced stock in various sauces.

2. The milk, lemon and herb stock can be used for sauces, or simple fish soups and stews. However, you can use it to poach or cook your fish. When this stock is reduced it becomes thick and rather syrupy in consistency and, among its many uses, it is the stock (or *fumet*) used in many of the classic sauces.

Stocks can be made in advance and kept in the refrigerator or frozen in an ice-cube tray and stored in the freezer. If you are not inclined to such forward planning it is a good idea to braise or poach your fish with the vegetables and fish trimmings surrounding the fish, and covered with wine, water or milk. Then you will also have a delicious and well flavoured liquid with which to continue making a sauce or dressing.

I am going to begin the basic sauce recipes with standard sauces that use the fish stock and are thickened with a roux (a mixture of flour and butter).

This Surimi Soup (page 84) and Hearty Fish Soup (page 81) show one of the many uses of good fish stock.

FISH VELOUTÉ

40 g / 1½ oz butter
40 g / 1½ oz flour
600 ml / 1 pint fish stock (page 170)

IN a heavy saucepan, melt the butter, add the flour and stir continuously for 2 minutes over a low heat. Gradually add the fish stock, stirring all the time (a balloon whisk is useful for this). Cook for 2 to 3 minutes on a low heat. This basic velouté can now be incorporated into many other sauces. MAKES 600 ML / 1 PINT

VARIATIONS

Green Sauce: Make the basic velouté sauce, then add a squeeze of lemon juice and 1 to 2 tablespoons well drained spinach purée. Beat in until smooth.

Summer Herb Sauce: Add 2 tablespoons finely chopped fresh green herbs to the velouté sauce. A little minced and cooked onion could be added, too.

White Wine and Parsley Sauce: Add 4 tablespoons white wine to the sauce and further reduce. Add 2 tablespoons finely chopped parsley and a knob or two of butter to enrichen.

Sauce Aurore: To a thick velouté sauce, add about 4 tablespoons of fresh tomato purée.

WHITE (OR BÉCHAMEL) SAUCES

The classic white sauce that everyone knows, is really a type of béchamel sauce. The roux of flour and butter (or margarine) is used to thicken the liquid of the sauce, which is always milk.

BASIC WHITE SAUCE

50 g / 2 oz flour
50 g / 2 oz butter or margarine
600 ml / 1 pint milk
pinch each of salt and pepper

IN a heavy saucepan, melt the butter, add the flour and stir continuously for 2 minutes over a low heat. Gradually add the milk, off the heat, stirring all the time. Cook over a low heat for 2 to 3 minutes as the sauce thickens. Season with the salt and pepper. MAKES 600 ML / 1 PINT

CLASSIC BÉCHAMEL

The above white sauce is a simplified version of béchamel sauce, which can accommodate many additional ingredients. But this béchamel is well worth taking a little trouble over for a 'special effort' sauce.

600 ml / 1 pint of milk
1 bay leaf
6 peppercorns
½ small onion or 1 shallot, finely sliced
40 g / 1½ oz butter or margarine
50 g / 2 oz flour
pinch of salt

PUT a pan of milk on a low heat, add the bay leaf, peppercorns and onion and infuse for about 8 minutes. Do not let the milk boil. Melt the butter in a heavy saucepan and stir in the flour. Cook for 1 to 2 minutes on a low heat, take off the heat and stir in the strained warm milk, whisking all the time to keep it smooth. Just simmer the sauce on a low heat for 1 to 2 minutes as the sauce thickens, then check the seasoning. A little top-of-the-milk or single cream could be added, if liked. MAKES 600 ML / 1 PINT

LOW-FAT WHITE SAUCE

40 g/1½ oz butter or margarine
40 g/1½ oz white or wholemeal flour
450 ml/¾ pint skimmed milk
1 blade mace (optional)
1 bay leaf
1 shallot, very finely chopped
salt and freshly ground black pepper

MELT the butter in a heavy saucepan, stir in the flour and cook for 2 minutes on a very low heat. Slide off the heat and gradually add the milk, using a whisk. Add the mace, bay leaf and shallot, return to the heat and bring up to just simmering. Cook for a further 10 minutes, stirring to prevent sticking and lumps. Season to taste when the sauce is ready. MAKES 450 ML/¾ PINT

VARIATIONS ON WHITE SAUCE

Parsley Sauce. Towards the end of cooking the sauce, throw in a good 2 tablespoons finely chopped parsley. Sharpen with a squeeze of lemon juice.

Mornay Sauce: Add 75–100 g/3–4 oz grated Gruyère or good Cheddar cheese. Alternatively, use 25 g/1 oz freshly grated Parmesan together with 50 g/2 oz grated Gruyère or Cheddar cheese. Stir into the sauce as it is thickening and continue stirring until all the cheese is melted and the sauce is smooth. Add 1 teaspoon prepared English mustard if you like.

Sauce Aurore: Add 150–300 ml/¼–½ pint of reduced pulp of fresh tomatoes (peeled, deseeded and mashed). You will need a thick basic white sauce for this, as the water in the tomatoes will thin it down. Add 1 to 2 teaspoons concentrated tomato purée if the tomatoes are lacking in colour and flavour.

Mushroom Sauce: Gently cook 100 g/4 oz sliced button mushrooms in a little butter or oil – do not let them brown. Add to the sauce in the finishing stage, with a pinch of cayenne.

Onion Sauce: Gently cook 450 g/1 lb finely chopped onion in a little butter or oil until soft, but not browned. Add to the basic white or béchamel sauce. If preferred, you can purée the onion first. Alternatively, you could simmer the chopped onion in a little fish stock, then purée in a food processor or blender and add to a thick white sauce for a smooth and flavoursome sauce.

Fennel Sauce: Finely chop the feathery leaves of fennel (or wild fennel) and add 2 tablespoons to the basic sauce. Continue simmering for 2 minutes to extract the aroma of the fennel.

Dill Sauce: Repeat as for the Fennel Sauce. Dill has a similar flavour to fennel but is not quite so strong and pungent.

Tarragon Sauce: Try to use the leaves of fresh tarragon, for the best flavour. Repeat as for Fennel Sauce and add a squeeze of fresh lemon juice.

Mild Curry Sauce: When you begin to make your white sauce, add 1 to 2 teaspoons curry powder to the melted butter and cook over a low heat for 30 seconds before adding the flour. Continue to make the sauce in the usual way. This is not a traditional Indian curry sauce but it does have a nice creamy taste.

Mustard Sauce: Add 2 to 3 teaspoons prepared English mustard, or wholegrain mustard, to the sauce and cook over a low heat for 30 seconds.

Anchovy Sauce: Add 6 pounded anchovy fillets, or a few drops of anchovy essence, to the basic white sauce.

Caper Sauce: Add 2 tablespoons capers to the basic white sauce.

Stuffed Sea Bream with Fennel Sauce (page 88) and Stuffed Squid with Tomato Sauce (page 125)

BASIC SAUCES USING VEGETABLE PURÉES

You can use most vegetables to make a suitable puréed sauce or accompaniment for fish. The vegetable can be lightly cooked in water, or braised in stock, then put into a food processor or blender with a little of the cooking juices and processed until smooth. You can then stir in a little fromage blanc, cream, or yogurt to make a smooth and creamy-textured sauce. The fresh colours of these sauces are a joy in themselves, and you can use your favourite herbs or spices to enliven them if you wish.

WATERCRESS SAUCE

2–3 bunches watercress
900 ml / 1½ pints water
pinch of salt
squeeze of fresh lemon juice
2 tablespoons fromage blanc or low-fat cream cheese

WASH and trim the watercress and cook briskly in boiling salted water for 2 minutes. Drain well and plunge into cold water, then drain again. Put the watercress into the bowl of a food processor or blender and purée until smooth. Then add the fromage blanc or cream cheese and process until smooth. You can gently re-heat this sauce or serve it chilled. MAKES 900 ML / 1½ PINTS

VARIATIONS
Spinach Sauce: Use the same method as for Watercress Sauce, substituting 450 g / 1 lb fresh spinach for the watercress.

Carrot Purée: Carrots need a longer cooking time before blending, with a little of their cooking water, to a smooth purée. Add a few finely chopped fresh herbs and stir in 2 to 3 tablespoons soured cream and a pinch of freshly ground black pepper.

FRESH TOMATO SAUCE

This fresh sauce is one of my favourites, and is extremely versatile. You can add more, or less, herbs of your own choice and taste to suit the personality of the recipe you are cooking. The carrot adds a little sweetness and colour to the sauce so do not omit it!

1 medium onion, finely chopped
1 clove garlic, crushed (optional)
2 teaspoons olive oil
1 medium carrot, grated
675 g / 1½ lb ripe tomatoes
1 teaspoon concentrated tomato purée
1 tablespoon chopped fresh herbs, such as basil, tarragon, or oregano
pinch each of salt and black pepper
a little wine (optional)

GENTLY cook the onion and garlic in the olive oil until softened. Add the carrot and cook for another 1 to 2 minutes. Peel the tomatoes and chop coarsely (see page 80). Add these and all the other ingredients to the pan. Bring up to just simmering and cook for about 10 minutes. Blend until smooth.

Cook for a longer time to reduce and thicken if you need this sauce to add to another sauce or dish. Add a little wine if you are in the mood – white or red. MAKES 600 ML / 1 PINT

COLD TOMATO SAUCE

*450 g / 1 lb fresh tomatoes, peeled, deseeded and
chopped (page 80)
1 clove garlic, crushed
150 ml / $\frac{1}{4}$ pint mayonnaise (page 181)
150 ml / $\frac{1}{4}$ pint soured cream
1 teaspoon concentrated tomato purée
$\frac{1}{2}$ teaspoon finely chopped fresh basil*

BLEND the tomatoes and garlic until smooth.
Then stir in the remaining combined in-
gredients and chill before serving. MAKES
ABOUT 600 ML / 1 PINT

SAFFRON SAUCE

*1 small onion or 2 shallots
150 ml / $\frac{1}{4}$ pint dry white wine
150 ml / $\frac{1}{4}$ pint double cream
pinch of saffron powder*

FINELY chop the onion or shallots and place
in a saucepan with the wine. Bring to the boil
and simmer until the wine is reduced to 1
tablespoon. Remove from the heat, stir in the
cream and saffron powder. MAKES ABOUT
150 ML / $\frac{1}{4}$ PINT

COLD SAFFRON SAUCE

This is a good sauce for shellfish and cold fish
dishes.

*150 ml / $\frac{1}{4}$ pint mayonnaise (page 181)
$\frac{1}{4}$ teaspoon saffron powder
squeeze of fresh lemon juice
150 ml / $\frac{1}{4}$ pint natural yogurt*

COMBINE all the ingredients and chill. MAKES
300 ML / $\frac{1}{2}$ PINT

FRUIT SAUCES

Fruit sauces are lovely with all fish. 'Tart' fruit such as rhubarb and gooseberries are particularly good with oily fish like mackerel and herring.

GOOSEBERRY SAUCE

225 g/8 oz gooseberries
a little water
a knob of butter
a little honey, to taste (optional)

WASH, top and tail the gooseberries and cook in a little water until tender. This quantity will reduce down to 150 ml/¼ pint. The sauce can be served like this or blend it into a smooth purée, and stir in the knob of butter. If it is very tart, add a teaspoon of honey. A tablespoon of yogurt, cream or fromage blanc can also be stirred in.

Another interesting option is to add 2 teaspoons of finely chopped mint. MAKES ABOUT 150 ML/¼ PINT

Mackerel with Gooseberry Sauce (above) and Marinated Herring with Blackberry Sauce (page 97)

RHUBARB SAUCE

350 g/12 oz rhubarb
a little water
squeeze of orange juice

WASH and cut up the rhubarb and cook in a little water until tender. Purée until smooth, and add a squeeze of fresh orange juice for extra piquancy. MAKES ABOUT 250 ML/ 8 FL OZ

VARIATIONS

Other fruit sauces can be made in the same way using blackberries, blackcurrants, redcurrants, and cranberries, and all these fruits are valuable for vitamins and minerals.

APPLE AND HORSERADISH SAUCE

225 g/8 oz Bramley or other cooking apples
4 tablespoons water
2 teaspoons honey
1 strip of lemon or orange peel
1 tablespoons horseradish sauce

PEEL and core the apples then cook in the water with the orange rind until the apples are a pulp. Add the honey to taste and stir in the horseradish sauce. MAKES ABOUT 150 ML/ ¼ PINT

HOLLANDAISE SAUCE

Hollandaise, Béarnaise, mousseline and related sauces are not thickened by flour but use the reduction method to concentrate flavour and are thickened with eggs and butter, or cream and butter. They are served warm rather than hot, and take a little patience and time to make. There are short cut methods using a liquidiser or blender, which are also given here.

HOLLANDAISE SAUCE

3 tablespoons white wine vinegar
2 tablespoons water
6 white peppercorns
100–175 g / 4–6 oz butter
3 egg yolks
squeeze of lemon juice
pinch of salt

PUT the vinegar, water and peppercorns into a small, heavy saucepan, bring to the boil and reduce the liquid to about 1 tablespoon. Strain the vinegar into a bowl and leave to cool. Meanwhile, melt the butter. Beat the egg yolks until frothy. Stand the bowl of vinegar over a pan of simmering water (making sure that the bowl does not touch the water), and beat in the egg yolks. Then, very gradually, add three quarters of the melted butter, stirring all the time until the sauce thickens and is of a creamy consistency. Add a squeeze of lemon juice and, if the sauce is too sharp, add a little of the reserved melted butter. If the mixture thickens too quickly as you are cooking, take away from the heat for a few seconds, before returning to the heat and continuing to beat. MAKES 300 ML / ½ PINT

BLENDER HOLLANDAISE SAUCE

4 egg yolks
2 tablespoons water
2 tablespoons lemon juice
175 g / 6 oz butter, melted
pinch each of salt and white pepper

PUT the egg yolks, water and lemon juice into a liquidiser or blender and turn on the power. While the machine is still running, pour in the melted butter until the sauce is thick. Season to taste. MAKES 300 ML / ½ PINT

BÉARNAISE SAUCE

The chervil and tarragon, when reduced, give a highly concentrated flavour to this sauce.

1 tablespoon finely chopped shallot
1 tablespoon finely chopped fresh tarragon
1 tablespoon finely chopped fresh chervil or parsley
4 tablespoons tarragon vinegar
4 tablespoons dry white wine
4 white peppercorns
175 g / 6 oz butter
3 large egg yolks
pinch each of salt and cayenne

PUT the shallot, tarragon, chervil (or parsley), vinegar, white wine and peppercorns in a heavy pan and cook briskly until the liquid is reduced to about 2 tablespoons. Strain the liquid and leave to cool.

Meanwhile, melt the butter and beat the eggs until frothy. Put the liquid into a bowl over a pan of barely simmering water and beat in the egg yolks. Add the butter gradually, stirring continuously, until the sauce is thick and creamy. Season to taste with the salt and cayenne. MAKES ABOUT 300 ML / ½ PINT

BLENDER BÉARNAISE SAUCE

1 tablespoon finely chopped shallot
2 tablespoons white wine vinegar
10 white peppercorns, bruised
3 egg yolks
1½ tablespoons lemon juice
150 g / 5 oz butter, melted
pinch each of salt and freshly ground black pepper

REDUCE the vinegar, onion and peppercorns by half in a heavy-based saucepan. Strain the liquid and leave to cool. Put the egg yolks and lemon juice into the liquidiser or blender and process until creamy, then pour in the strained vinegar. With the machine still running, pour the melted butter in slowly until all is thickened to a creamy sauce. Season to taste. MAKES ABOUT 150 ML/¼ PINT

MAYONNAISE

To my mind, this is one of the most enjoyable sauces to make by hand. A lot has been made of the method and mystique (will it thicken – will it separate?), and yet if all the ingredients are at room temperature, and the eggs are more than three days old, and the mixing bowl is perfectly dry, you should not have any problem!

Blenders are invaluable for quick method mayonnaise and with hand-made or blender mayonnaise there are endless uses of, and additions to, this sauce.

2 egg yolks
½ teaspoon Dijon mustard
300 ml / ½ pint good olive or sunflower oil
1–2 tablespoons white wine vinegar
pinch each of salt and white pepper
pinch of cayenne (optional)
squeeze of lemon juice

PUT the egg yolks and mustard into a small mixing bowl (I like to stand the bowl on a damp dish-cloth or tea-towel to stop it slipping around while beating and adding the oil). Beat with a small wooden spoon until the yolks are creamy. As you are beating, stir in the oil drop by drop, increasing to a steady trickle as the mayonnaise thickens.

Keep beating all the time. (If the mayonnaise separates, take another egg yolk and beat it in another basin, then slowly add to the separated mixture, beating all the time, until it thickens and becomes smooth again.)

When all the oil has been incorporated, add the vinegar – the mayonnaise will lighten in colour immediately. Season with salt and pepper, add a pinch of cayenne, if liked, and a squeeze of lemon juice. MAKES JUST OVER 300 ML/½ PINT

BLENDER MAYONNAISE

2 egg yolks or 2 whole eggs
½ teaspoon of Dijon mustard or pinch of mustard powder
2 tablespoons white wine vinegar or 3 tablespoons lemon juice
300 ml/½ pint olive or sunflower oil
salt and freshly ground black pepper

PUT the egg yolks (or whole eggs), mustard and 1 tablespoon of white wine vinegar into the bowl of a liquidiser or blender and process for 20 seconds.

With the machine still running, add the oil slowly through the feed tube and continue for 1 minute until the mayonnaise is thick and smooth. Add the remaining white wine vinegar and season to taste, process for 10 seconds. MAKES JUST OVER 300 ML/½ PINT

VARIATIONS ON MAYONNAISE

Mayonnaise can be thinned down with natural yogurt, fromage blanc, soured cream, single cream or milk to use as a simple dressing.

Other simple flavourings, among the endless possibilities, could be: finely chopped herbs – fennel leaves, snipped chives, chopped chervil or parsley, tarragon or coriander leaves, capers, chopped gherkins, or chopped peeled cooked prawns. You could also whip in prepared horseradish or tartare sauce.

There are so many variations based on mayonnaise that are perfect accompaniments with fish, and I particularly like a mixture of mayonnaise, natural yogurt, thinned down with 1 to 2 tablespoons fish stock and flavoured with appropriate herbs.

Salmon in Aspic, with Mayonnaise (page 137)

Tartare Sauce: Add 1 teaspoon finely chopped gherkins, 1 teaspoon finely chopped capers, 1 teaspoon fresh chopped herbs, and ½ teaspoon Dijon mustard to 150 ml/¼ pint mayonnaise.

Curry Flavoured Mayonnaise: Add ½ teaspoon ground coriander, ½ teaspoon ground cumin and ¼ teaspoon ground turmeric to the egg yolks just before making the mayonnaise and continue in the normal way. Then add 1 to 2 tablespoons natural yogurt. Alternatively, add 1–2 teaspoons curry powder to the prepared mayonnaise.

Cocktail Sauce: To 150 ml/¼ pint home-made mayonnaise, add 1 tablespoon concentrated tomato purée, a dash of Tabasco sauce and a squeeze of lemon juice. Season with salt and pepper to taste. You could add finely chopped fresh basil instead of the Tabasco sauce.

Prawn Cocktail (page 77)

AÏOLI

This is the famous garlic mayonnaise of Provence.

6 cloves garlic
pinch each of salt and freshly ground
black pepper
2 egg yolks
300 ml/½ pint olive oil
squeeze of lemon juice

YOU can use a little less garlic, according to your taste or the strength and size of the garlic cloves. Peel the cloves, and pound them in a basin, with a pinch of salt, until they are thoroughly mashed. Then add the egg yolks and beat with a wooden spoon. Add the oil drop by drop, beating all the time and continue until the sauce thickens and all the oil is incorporated. When the mixture is creamy, add a squeeze of fresh lemon juice and pepper to taste. MAKES 300 ML/½ PINT

VINAIGRETTE DRESSING

3 tablespoons olive or sunflower oil
1 tablespoon white wine vinegar
½ teaspoon Dijon mustard
pinch each of salt and pepper

PUT all the ingredients together in a screw-top jar and shake vigorously to combine.

VARIATIONS

Lemon Dressing: Substitute 1 tablespoon lemon juice for the vinegar in the Vinaigrette Dressing. This dressing is particularly suitable when drinking wine with the meal.

Herb Dressing: Add 1 tablespoon chopped fresh herbs to either the Vinaigrette or the Lemon Dressing.

Garlic Dressing: Add 1–2 crushed garlic cloves to the Vinaigrette or Lemon Dressing.

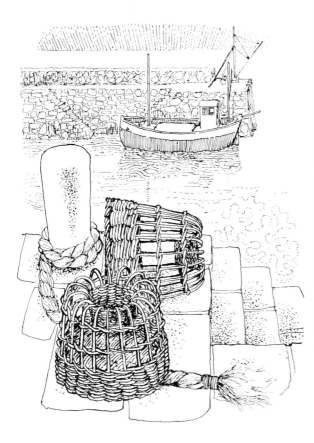

SAVOURY BUTTERS

Take a freshly grilled, poached or baked fish and add a suspicion of melting savoury butter and you will have a succulent and delectable fish dish. All these flavourings are for 100 g/4 oz butter, and liquidisers and blenders are very useful for making them. Use only a tiny knob of butter for flavouring white fish (it is unnecessary for oily fish). The fish should *not* be served swimming in butter.

MAÎTRE D'HÔTEL BUTTER

Illustrated on pages 186–7

100 g/4 oz butter, softened
2 tablespoons finely chopped parsley
½ teaspoon lemon juice
pinch each of salt and freshly ground black pepper

BEAT the butter until creamy, then add the chopped parsley, lemon juice and seasoning to taste. Form into a roll, chill and cut slices of this butter as required.

VARIATIONS

Lemon Butter: Add 1 teaspoon grated lemon rind plus a squeeze of lemon juice, to the softened butter. Use the same method for Lime Butter.

Green Butter: Finely chop 2 tablespoons fresh summer herbs and add to the softened butter.

Mint Butter: Add 2 tablespoons chopped fresh mint to the softened butter.

Shrimp or Prawn Butter: Pound 1 to 2 tablespoons peeled cooked shrimps or prawns to a paste and beat into the butter.

Garlic Butter: Beat 2 cloves crushed garlic and 2 teaspoons snipped chives into the butter.

Anchovy Butter: This is very good spread on water biscuits or toast and baked until crisp. Pound 4 to 6 anchovy fillets to a smooth paste and beat this, or a few drops of anchovy essence, into the butter.

Crab or Lobster Butter: Use 2 tablespoons flaked crab meat (or the pounded red roe from the female of the crab) or the coral and roe from the lobster and beat into the butter. This butter is also good for enriching soups or sauces.

Tomato Butter: Add 2 tablespoons concentrated tomato purée, or fresh tomato pulp, to the softened butter, add a squeeze of fresh lemon juice and a pinch of freshly ground black pepper.

Anise Butter: Use 1 tablespoon Pernod or Ricard beaten into the softened butter.

Rum Butter: 1 tablespoon rum beaten into softened butter. This is a very good, if unusual, accompaniment for fish.

ALL-PURPOSE GENERAL BATTER

You can adjust the consistency of this batter by adding more or less liquid to the flour.

100 g/4 oz plain flour
pinch of salt
3 tablespoons olive oil
250 ml/8 fl oz water or beer
1–2 egg whites

SIFT the flour into a bowl and add a pinch of salt. Make a well in the centre, add the oil and, using a balloon whisk or wooden spoon, beat the oil in. Add the water gradually, beating from the outside of the bowl towards the centre. Just before using, whisk the egg white(s) and fold into the batter.

ALL-PURPOSE LIGHT BATTER

This is based on the Japanese tempura batter. It is light and crisp, and simple to make.

1 egg, lightly beaten
250 ml/8 fl oz water
100 g/4 oz white flour, sifted

COMBINE all the ingredients with a balloon whisk or fork, and beat lightly for a short time. It does not need the lengthy beating of other batter mixtures.

BLENDER BATTER

100 g/4 oz plain flour, sifted
1 egg
pinch of salt
5 tablespoons milk

PUT all the ingredients into the bowl of a liquidiser or blender and process until smooth – about 45 seconds. The amount of liquid can be adjusted according to the recipe requirements.

Megrim Fillets with Citrus Marinade (page 72), Salmon with Maître d'Hôtel Butter (page 184) and Deep-Fried Monkfish in Apple Batter (page 76)

MARINADES

As I have already mentioned, the flesh of fish is naturally tender and (with the exception of octopus!) does not need beating, bashing, boiling or marinating to tenderise it further.

So the usual purpose behind marinating fish is to impregnate the flesh with subtle infusions of aromatic or rather more pungent flavours, and it is particularly good for fish which has a mild flavour. A marinade can also enhance and emphasise the flavour of more superior fish, and helps to keep the flesh from drying out when cooked by the high heat of a grill, barbecue, or oven.

Marinades are a combination of herbs and spices, maybe a little sliced shallot, garlic, wine or cider, oil or yogurt, vinegar or juice from citrus fruits, mustard, soy sauce, tomato purée, Worcestershire sauce – the combinations and variations are endless. Sometimes the ingredients for a marinade can be cooked first to extract the flavours and aroma, as in Chilled Marinated Cod Steaks (see page 89). Marinades containing citrus juice can be used to 'cook' raw fish, as in Sashimi and Ceviche (see pages 65 and 141). The liquid from the marinade can be used for brushing or basting while the fish is cooking – and can also be incorporated in a sauce or dressing for the finished dish.

The tender flesh of fish is in danger of becoming soggy and flaky if it is marinated for too long. As a rule, no more than 4 hours for a whole fish, a little less for fillets, and 30 minutes or so for bite-sized pieces of fish like monkfish and scallops, is all that is necessary.

Use a glass or earthenware dish for marinating, and turn the fish from time to time. With a whole fish, it is a good idea to make criss-cross slashes along the body so that the marinating mixture or paste can fully penetrate the flesh. Brush or spread the marinade into the cuts and remember to turn the fish two or three times while it sits in a cool place for 3 or 4 hours.

Yet another use of marinades is for pickling, spicing, or sousing fish. This is a good method for oily varieties as the acid of the marinade offsets the richness of the fish and is helpful in softening the small bones of tiny fish like pilchards, sardines and sprats. Many spiced or pickled fish dishes are best kept for three or four days before eating – and will in fact keep for some time. The simple procedure for Gravad Lax (see page 64) produces an exquisitely flavoured salmon dish, but can be used with equal success for the more humble mackerel. Remember, fish is a versatile food, so do substitute marinade ingredients and varieties of fish, and also shellfish, according to season and availability. Be adventurous!

Glossary

Bass (Sea Bass) – is sometimes known as salmon bass although it does not belong to the salmon family. It is a most handsome silvery fish, with beautiful lean white flesh, and is best stuffed and baked whole, though steaks of bass are excellent when grilled or barbecued.

Bream (Sea Bream) – another superb fish, is known as *dourade* in France, where it is very popular. Excellent when poached, baked or grilled.

Brill – a flat fish of good flavour, which I think is best cooked on the bone, using recipes also suitable for turbot.

Catfish – a strange looking fish with a blunt head and firm flesh. You will usually find only the fillets for sale in your fishmongers. The catfish is also known as wolf fish, which will give you some idea of its fierce appearance.

Cockles – the great seaside favourite, this bi-valve should be cooked for about 6 minutes: then the cockle is easily removed from the shell. Cockles give a lovely flavour to fish soups and sauces, and they can, of course, also be eaten raw with vinegar.

Cod – is a marvellously versatile fish with a high nutritional value, which can be cooked by any method. Smoked cod's roe can be used in fish sauces, for making taramasalata, or simply grilled on toast.

Coley – also known as saithe and coalfish, a member of the cod family, tough with darker coloured flesh which turns white when cooked. It is usually sold in fillets and can be used for any recipe calling for cod, haddock or pollack.

Conger Eel – gaining in popularity again, this marine eel has a good strong flavour and firm flesh, making it ideal for braises and pies. Smoked conger eel makes a delicious starter or salad.

Crab – of the many species of crab around our shores, the large common crab is the one we usually see on sale in Britain. But spider crab and the blue swimming crabs are worth looking for when on holiday – they can be cooked and used in the same way as the common crab.

Crawfish – also known as spiny lobster. The crawfish is a 'lobster red' colour *before* it is cooked, whereas live lobster is a beautiful, slatey-blue colour and turns red only after boiling. The other main difference between these two crustaceans is that the crawfish does not have the huge main claws of the lobster.

Dab – available whole or filleted, dab is a good economical flat fish which can be used in many recipes calling for inexpensive flat fish.

Flounder – a flat fish which can be cooked whole or filleted.

Gurnard (Red Gurnard) – is not a very prepossessing fish to look at, with its large, strangely shaped bony head, but its firm white and slightly dry flesh is well worth eating. It can be cooked whole, or you can lift off the fillets first and use the head and carcass for stock or soup. The gurnard family also includes the grey and the yellow gurnard, which can be cooked in the same way.

Haddock – a member of the cod family and considered by many to be superior. It has a distinctive thumb print on each side, supposedly representing the mark of the finger and thumb of St Peter. The roe is a great delicacy and is very popular in France.

Hake – another member of the cod family and a favourite fish of mine. It has very white, firm flesh, is easily boned and can be bought whole or in fillets and cutlets. It can be used for most white fish recipes.

Halibut – the largest of all the flat fish (the maximum length of a halibut can be 3 metres/10 feet). Fillets or steaks of halibut should be cooked in lightly buttered aluminium foil, brushed with an oil-based marinade or a little melted savoury butter, as the flesh tends to be dry. Chicken halibut (the young, smaller fish) can be cooked like sole.

Herring – the name herring comes from the Teutonic word 'Heer' meaning army. This is very appropriate as a shoal of these beautiful fish, with their streamlined bodies built for speed, may cover a vast area and contain many thousands, if not millions, of fish! Herring is a very nutritious fish and is a particularly rich source of protein, fat, iodine and vitimins A and D. Oily fish like herring are excellent to grill or barbeque.

Huss – also known as dogfish, flake or rigg, is a cartilaginous (i.e. non-bony) fish and is, in fact, a species of shark. It is a good all-purpose fish, usually bought skinned. Their skins are so tough that they were actually used in the past for polishing wood and alabaster!

John Dory – in my part of the world the fishermen call John Dory 'handbags'. It is an extraordinary fish to behold, and you can indeed carry it like a handbag, which is the best way to pick one up and avoid the very sharp spines – there is a ridge which forms a sort of handle in the upper curve of the fish. The head is very bony and the mouth has a fascinating feature of being able swiftly to extend to engulf its prey. Like haddock, it has the distinctive thumb prints of St Peter. The carcass makes excellent stock when you lift off the lovely firm white fillets, or you can bake or grill it whole. The taste is exceptionally good.

Ling – the largest of the cod family, growing to a maximum length of 2 metres/6 feet. The liver is rich in oil and the white flesh has a good texture and flavour and can be cooked like cod. It may also be possible to find dried and salted ling, which can be pre-soaked like cod and used in the same way.

Lobster – live lobster are a beautiful slatey-blue colour, turning to a pinky red when cooked. Their flesh is so succulent and superior in taste that I think that they are often best served with a simple salad and wedges of lemon. They do tend to be expensive but, because the meat is so rich and filling, a small portion of lobster for each person is all that is required.

Mackerel – a brilliant dark greeny-blue back with an irregular pattern of still darker zig-zag lines are the beautiful and familiar features of this versatile and delicious oily fish. Grill it, bake it or souse it for wonderful dishes. Smoked mackerel is very popular and, as with all oily fish, tart fruit sauces are an excellent accompaniment and help offset the richness of the flesh.

Megrim – this fish will need a little extra flavouring – for instance a piquant marinade or a cheese sauce – as this flat fish can be rather dry and lacking in any distinctive flavour of its own.

Monkfish (Anglerfish) – the flesh of monkfish is superb in taste and texture and is faintly reminiscent of lobster. It can be cooked in a great variety of ways – poached, baked, stewed, grilled or fried and happily is becoming more widely available in this country. The strange and ugly head of monkfish is rarely seen as only the tail end is sold. Incidentally, the whole tail can be roasted (rather like a leg of lamb) with oil, lemon, garlic and rosemary. Bone it first, or not, as you please. A most wonderfully delicious fish.

Mullet, Grey – the flesh of grey mullet has a beautiful flavour, and in my view is very much under-rated. It can be cooked and served in many ways but is particularly good when stuffed and baked whole. Remember that it needs scaling before cooking.

Mullet, Red – a summer visitor to British waters, and very pretty and welcome it is too! It is a fish valued highly for its taste and appearance and is usually cooked intact to give more flavour: the liver is a delicacy. Grilling or baking are the best cooking methods for the delicate flesh of this fish.

Mussels – this shellfish deserves more praise: they are cheap, very tasty, and their cooking juices contribute a lovely distinctive flavour to all seafood dishes and soups.

Norway Lobster – also known as nephrop, Dublin Bay prawns, scampi and langoustine, belongs to the same family as the lobster. The tails can be deep fried and served as scampi, or served cold with salad and mayonnaise. Whole shellfish look beautiful served on a bed of crushed ice and, although a rather fiddly finger food, the meat in the claws is well worth getting at.

Oysters – there are three species of oyster which form the basis of the industry in Britain: the European flat oyster, the Portuguese oyster and, more recently, the Pacific or Japanese oyster. You must be an expert to differentiate between them. Oysters are a good source of minerals, particularly zinc. The farming of oysters has brought down the price within the scope of the average household budget.

Plaice – a good flat fish with a most attractively coloured skin. Small plaice are best served on the bone. Lift off the thick, white fillets of larger plaice and use in a variety of recipes.

Pollack – is often called a poor relation to the cod, but I think it is a very useful and tasty fish. It can be cooked in the same way as cod and haddock. It is good for basic pies and made-up dishes such as rissoles, croquettes and fish cakes.

Salmon – a magnificent fish which is prized by all. Experts differ in their opinion over the taste of farmed or wild salmon (and salmon trout) but for most people, salmon is a rather special fish reserved for special occasions. Smoked salmon and Gravad Lax (see page 64) are often served as a starter.

Scallops and Queens – the white flesh of the scallop, with its pinky-orange coral, is a most tender and tasty meat, as too is the much smaller queen. Both shells (or valves) of the queen are rounded, as compared to the great scallop which has one flat and one rounded shell. Scallops – whether grilled, lightly sautéed, or poached – must always be cooked tenderly and quickly or the flesh may become tough. Queens need the same treatment and are also good to use as a stuffing for other varieties of fish.

Shrimp – the shrimp, which is commonly found in shallow water around the British coast, is often called or mistaken for the prawn. Shrimps make a delightful little mouthful when eaten whole, as they are in France. In Britain they are more often cunningly incorporated into sauces, soups, rissottos, salads and stews.

Skate – the wonderful wings of skate with their beautiful shades of colour have a good taste, and the texture of the fish is very similar to crab. It deserves to be carefully poached in a well-flavoured stock or wine, or it can be shallow fried.

Sole, Dover – a flat fish of superb quality, the flavour of which should never be masked by too-rich sauces or flavourings. It is best to poach or grill this magnificent creature carefully and serve it with wedges of lemon and the minimum of fuss. The Dover sole is actually the only true sole and belongs to a different family to that of the lemon sole, but both fish can be cooked whole or in fillets, and respond to the same cooking methods.

Sole, Lemon – a very good flat fish. It has a lovely flavour and many classic recipes are attributable to lemon sole. I prefer it grilled or baked on the bone.

Sprat – the delicious little sprat, also canned and known as brisling or Swedish anchovies, is often thought to be young herring. In fact, it is a distinct species and easily recognised by its bluey-green back, silvery sides and belly. Absolutely smashing for barbecueing, grilling, frying, baking and stuffing.

Squid – this mollusc has a torpedo-shaped body with a transparent inner shell. It is a cephalopod, which literally means 'head footed' and refers to the way in which the arms and tentacles sprout directly from the head. It is an excellent and delicious seafood, and easier to prepare than you might imagine.

Trout – fresh trout, to be cooked in newspaper, grilled, sautéed or poached, is widely available in most fishmongers' and supermarkets. It can be cooked in a microwave as well as in all the traditional ways.

Turbot – along with Dover sole this fish has the most exquisite flavour of all the flat fish: the flesh is firm, meaty yet tender and juicy. The head and bones are a rich source of gelatine and are excellent used as a base for stocks and sauces. Steaks or fillets of turbot can be grilled, sautéed or poached and, although I think this fish is best served very simply, recipes for sole and other flat fish can be used. A young turbot – called chicken turbot – should be cooked whole, on the bone, if possible.

Whelks – like the cockle and winkle, whelks are very popular fare in pubs and stalls at the seaside. However, they can be rather tough if overcooked. They are good dipped in malt vinegar and for flavouring soups and stocks.

Whiting – yet another member of the cod family, and always in plentiful and cheap supply. Use in all recipes calling for white fish, but bear in mind that the flesh is inclined to be rather dry so grilling is better avoided.

Winkles – children love to pick out winkles with pins: they are great fun to hunt for on holiday. They have a fresh salty taste, and should be cooked like cockles.

Witch – also known as Torbay sole, can be confused with sole. A very good and tasty fish which can be cooked in the same way as all the other flat fish.

Wrasse – I mention wrasse because one day you may come across this bony fish, which is often just used as bait. However, in some countries, it is eaten with great relish and the situation may change in Britain. It would, at least, add wonderful flavour to soups or stews.

Index